DATE DUE

AP 29 '94			
SE 18 '97			
MR 2 '99			
MY 9 '02			

DEMCO 38-296

PIANO MUSIC
BY
BLACK WOMEN
COMPOSERS

Rippling Spring Waltz by Estelle D. Ricketts of Darby, Pennsylvania. 1893. Earliest published solo piano music by a black woman composer located to date. Library of Congress, Music Division.

PIANO MUSIC
BY
BLACK WOMEN
COMPOSERS

*A Catalog of Solo
and Ensemble Works*

Helen Walker-Hill

Music Reference Collection, Number 35

Greenwood Press
New York • Westport, Connecticut • London

Library of Congress Cataloging-in-Publication Data

Walker-Hill, Helen.
   Piano music by Black women composers : a catalog of solo and
ensemble works / Helen Walker-Hill.
      p.   cm.—(Music reference collection, ISSN 0736-7740 ; no.
35)
   Includes bibliographical references and index.
   Discography
   ISBN 0-313-28141-6 (alk. paper)
   1. Piano music—Bibliography.   2. Chamber music—Bibliography.
3. Piano music (Jazz)—Bibliography.   4. Afro-American women
composers—Bibliography.   5. Women composers, Black—Bibliography.
I. Title. II. Series.
ML128.P3W3   1992
016.7862′089′96073—dc20   91-38146

British Library Cataloguing in Publication Data is available.

Library of Congress Catalog Card Number: 91-38146
ISBN: 0-313-28141-6
ISSN: 0736-7740

First published in 1992

Greenwood Press, 88 Post Road West, Westport, CT 06881
An imprint of Greenwood Publishing Group, Inc.

Printed in the United States of America

The paper used in this book complies with the
Permanent Paper Standard issued by the National
Information Standards Organization (Z39.48-1984).

10 9 8 7 6 5 4 3 2 1

To all the composers whose music is recognized here

Contents

Preface

This catalog has its origins in the author's own need for such a resource in her piano teaching and performing. It is intended to provide practical assistance to other teachers and performers, and also to be useful to scholars and researchers seeking to assess the contributions of black women.

While music by some white women composers is gradually becoming available and the work of black male composers is also better known, that of black female composers remains the least accessible. Mildred Denby Green's book *Black Women Composers: A Genesis*, published in 1983, has been the most readily available resource on Florence Price, Margaret Bonds, Lena McLin, Evelyn Pittman, and Eva Jessye. A search of past issues of the periodical *Black Perspective in Music* yields a few more: Barbara Garvey Jackson's article on Florence Price, D. Antoinette Handy's on Mary Lou Williams, Carl Harris's on Undine Smith Moore, and Kathryn Talalay's on Philippa Duke Schuyler. Determined searching is required to locate what little information is available on other composers. The music listed, especially if instrumental music, is impossible to obtain through the usual channels—music stores and music libraries. Most of it is out of print or in unavailable manuscripts. It is evident that resources are needed which report existing music and how to obtain it.

Some significant black women composers will not be found listed in this catalog because the criteria for inclusion were necessarily narrow. It contains only nonvocal piano music because it was impossible to do justice to the large amount of vocal music. Therefore, those composers are excluded whose output consists only of works involving the voice (i.e., songs, arrangements of spirituals, and choral works). The many outstanding art songs and works for piano ensemble including voice, for instance, will require another project.

In addition, for the music listed to be useful to other performers, it was necessary for it to be written down. This excludes many composers of improvised piano music—Lovie Austin, Arizona Dranes, and Lillian Hardin Armstrong, among others. Where we are fortunate enough to have some written examples of the work of jazz composers Mary Lou Williams, Hazel Scott, Dorothy Donegan, and Valerie Capers, they have been happily included.

Furthermore, although this work is not limited to Afro-American women composers (two Afro-British composers are included), no special effort has been made to seek composers from other continents because information is too difficult to obtain. This catalog is not intended to represent the majority of black women's music. What remains here can be seen as a fraction, but also a potent distillation and indication, of their creative talent.

The composers and music were found through reading primary and secondary resources, researching collections and libraries' holdings (see **Acknowledgments**), conducting voluminous correspondence and extensive telephone inquiries, and personal interviews of musicians and composers in Chicago, Denver, New York, Philadelphia, and Washington, D.C.

The difficulties have been considerable. Because of the impropriety of women as public figures in the past and the lack of attention to the work of women composers, the available resources usually provide sketchy and often misleading information. Further obstacles have been presented by the necessity of relying upon word-of-mouth information, the difficulty of locating many composers, non-response by some of them and desire for privacy of others or their heirs. The wish of a few composers not to list their birth dates has been respected. Therefore, this work is necessarily incomplete and certainly includes errors. Readers, and the many composers who have not yet been located, are invited to supply further information by contacting the author through Greenwood Press.

It was decided to include music which is listed in bibliographic resources but is not (yet) located or accessible, so that we can have an idea as to the amount and kind of compositions that have existed for the piano and give credit where it is due. Another reason for its inclusion is the hope that information leading to its recovery may come forth.

The **Introduction** attempts to relate the work of black women composers to that of other composers, black and white, and to the accomplishments by black women in other fields. It also gives an overview of the history of black women composers.

The **Sources and Abbreviations** section lists the sources consulted which are relevant to more than one composer. Additional references are given at the end of the entry for individual composers on whom material is available, and a **Selected Bibliography** is located after the **Appendixes**.

The **Catalog of Solo and Ensemble Works** begins with a brief guide to its use, and lists the composers alphabetically. Their entries include a biographical sketch and description of their musical output, an address where their works can be obtained (if available), a list of their piano works with brief descriptions, and at the end, the sources of the information.

The **Appendixes** have been designed to increase the usefulness of the catalog for specific purposes. They include a list of published piano works readily available, a list of instrumentation to make it easier to find piano ensemble music for a given combination of instruments, a list of easy and moderate pieces for teaching purposes, and a chronological break-down of the few surviving piano works published or composed before 1920 for those desiring historical information.

The **Selected Bibliography** lists the books with the most extensive inclusion and discussion of black women composers, as well as articles and dissertations on individual composers.

The **Selected Discography** includes information on recordings of the listed piano music, as well as references to some recordings of other types of music by the composers in this catalog. It does not include recordings of jazz, blues, rock, popular, gospel, choral, and religious music by black women composers not listed here.

Acknowledgments

I wish to thank the Newberry Library and the University of Colorado for funding which supported the research for this project, and Dr. William Kearns for his gracious invitation to house the collected music in the American Music Research Center at the College of Music of the University of Colorado at Boulder.

This catalog owes its existence to the network of scholars, librarians, composers, and friends and relatives of composers who contributed references, names, addresses, titles, anecdotes, recollections of performances, and actual scores of music. I am especially indebted to Mildred Denby Green, Barbara Garvey Jackson, D. Antoinette Handy, Rae Linda Brown, and Kathryn Talalay for their ground-breaking scholarship on individual women composers and for their assistance to my research. Wayne Shirley at the Library of Congress Music Division provided invaluable information on music from before 1920. Assistance, large and small, but all significant, came from Ellistine Holly at Jackson State University in Mississippi, Wendell P. Whalum at Morehouse College, Deborra Richardson and Esme Bahn at the Moorland-Spingarn Research Center of Howard University, Patricia Turner at the Wilson Library of the University of Minnesota, Eero Richmond at the American Music Center in New York City, Agatha Kalkanis at the Detroit Public Library, Charlene Kaufmann at the University of Arkansas Libraries Special Collections, Janice Misurell Mitchell and Patricia Morehead of American Women Composers, Inc. in Chicago, Bonnie Hedges of American Women Composers in Washington, D.C., Morris Phibbs of the Center for Black Music Research at Columbia College in Chicago, Mary Yearwood at the Schomburg Center for Research in Black Culture in New York City, Richard Jackson at the New York Public Library, Ed Manney at the Vivian Harsh Research Collection in Chicago, Archie Motley at the

Chicago Historical Society, Laurel Boeckman at the State Historical Society of Missouri, Patricia Willis at the Yale University Beinecke Rare Books Collection, Harold Samuel at the Yale University Music Library, Nancy Shawcross at the University of Pennsylvania Van Pelt Library, Bob Heriard at the University of New Orleans Earl K. Long Library, Walter Moss of the Philadelphia chapter of the National Association of Negro Musicians, Rawn Spearman at the University of Lowell, Massachusetts, and Lance Bowling at Cambria Records and Publishing in Los Angeles. Special thanks go to Buckner Gamby at Virginia State University for sharing piano scores of Undine Smith Moore. Several friends and relatives of Margaret Bonds gave depth to the facts of her life: her daughter Djane Richardson in New York City, Nematilda Ritchie Woodard and Renée Lubell in Chicago, as well as Albert McNeil in Los Angeles. Theodore Charles Stone, Hortense Love, and Helen White in Chicago added information on both Florence Price and Margaret Bonds. And most of all, I am indebted to the many composers who were willing to share themselves and their music.

Bob Hill and Dianne Dugaw bore up my courage to begin this project, as did Carrie Collins, President of Rocky Mountain Musicians Association of the National Association of Negro Musicians, Inc. I am grateful to Mary Blair at Greenwood Press for her positive response to the project and for her patience. Eileen Cline extended her hospitality for several weeks during my research in Washington, D.C. Mike Noe contributed his expertise in selecting a personal computer. Chris Bogard-Reynolds of Document Prep desktop publishing in Denver prepared the camera-ready copy. I could not have completed the work without the moral support, objective judgement, and editorial assistance of Theresa Bogard.

Introduction

"When I was a young girl, I thought composers were white, male, and dead." Composer Dorothy Rudd Moore's *bon mot* rings ruefully true for most of us. However, despite major recording companies, symphony orchestras, and concert artists who still cling to the standard repertory, more and more non-white, female, and living composers are now heard on radio, recordings and concert programs.

African-American women composers are also beginning to receive recognition. We may be familiar with some of the close to three hundred identified songwriters in the blues, jazz, popular and gospel idioms—Bessie Smith, Mary Lou Williams, Natalie Cole, or Mahalia Jackson, for instance. We are less likely to have heard of any of the sixty to seventy known composers who have contributed symphonic works, operas, choral, chamber, vocal, and instrumental pieces. Although the music of a few of these composers is being published, most of their music unfortunately remains in manuscript. Music for piano is among the most difficult to find in print. However, as this catalog demonstrates, it is a large and significant body of literature. The current awakening of interest in the music of these composers should do much to insure its survival.

Compared to our day, the situation of black women composers in the past was even more problematic. Until recently, scholars paid little, if any, attention to women composers, and their activities were not recorded. Information is therefore scarce, and actual evidence in the form of written music is almost nonexistent. Much musical activity of women was anonymous. As is true today, many women who arranged and composed for their church choirs were unlikely to see their music in print. Manuscripts disappeared as composers died, and all that we have from before 1900 is a small amount of published sheet music. Were the compositions of present-day black women composers to suffer a similar fate, the impression of future historians based upon published music would be highly inaccurate.

While it is not surprising, it is nevertheless a keen disappointment to find very few actual scores of music from the nineteenth century when there are so many examples of literary work by black women, as well as works of art and a multitude of other accomplishments. In literature, Phyllis Wheatley (1753–1784) became the first black author to publish a book of poetry in 1773, followed by a series of "first" publications for the race by black women authors: Ann Plato's (b. 1820s?) *Essays,* in 1841, and Harriet Wilson's (1807?–1870) novel, the autobiographical *Our Nig,* in 1858. Black women continued to write unabated, and we have the publications of Frances Ellen Harper (1825–1911), Anna Julia Cooper (1859–1964), Alice Dunbar-Nelson 1875–1935), and a host of others. Some followed European and white American literary models, but many wrote of their own experiences and argued the abolitionist cause.

In art, the remarkable affinity for sculpture first demonstrated by Edmonia Lewis (1843–1909?) in the 1860s was followed by Meta Warrick Fuller (1877–1968), May Howard Jackson (1877–1931), Nancy Elizabeth Prophet (1887–?), and Augusta Savage (1892–1962). In painting, Annie Walker (1855–1929) set early standards of excellence. At first, these black women artists adopted the subjects and stylistic approach of European art and (in contrast to authors and composers) most of them studied in Europe.

Long before they became known as composers, black women achieved musical distinction as performers, studying in Europe and appearing on stage. A long list of celebrated singers stretches back to soprano Elizabeth Taylor Greenfield (1824–1876), Philadelphia's "Black Swan," who sang a command performance for the Queen of England, through the Hyers sisters, Anna (ca. 1853–193?) and Emma (ca. 1855–189?), Selika Williams (ca. 1849–1937), Sissieretta Jones (the "Black Patti," 1868–1933), and numerous others. Although a number of black men had careers as instrumentalists, it was not until much later that Hazel Harrison (1883–1969), who studied in Berlin with Feruccio Busoni and Egon Petri, became the first black female concert pianist to develop an international reputation.

These achievements coincided with the African-American struggle for self-improvement and equality that had been in progress in the North since well before the Civil War. Women figured prominently in this movement. The Afric-American Female Intelligence Society had been formed in Boston in 1832, the Philadelphia Library Company of Colored Persons was established in 1833, and by the 1850s, New York City had two black literary societies for women. Oberlin was the first college to admit black women, and the first to graduate was Mary Jane Patterson in 1862, followed by educator Frances Jackson Coppin in 1865 and many others.

In its striving for education and respectability, the black middle class took as its model the white society which surrounded it, along with many of its questionable values. One of these was the trivialization of the role of women. It is true that black women were not as dominated by society's narrow view of women's functions, and many of them were able to overcome this obstacle to achieve in a number of fields of endeavor. However, as we shall see, it did have its effect in the area of musical composition. The reasons for this are not clear. They probably have to do with the subtle, mysterious and powerful psychological effect of music which makes its creation, like religious authority, too dangerous to allow in the hands of women. The late composer Undine Smith Moore, in a talk to the First International Congress of Women in Music in New York City in 1981, alluded to the complexity of the issue and speculated on possible causes: the traditional male roles of authority as conductors and composers, the absorption of women's lives in the minutia of daily living, and the deep-seated prejudices regarding women's capacity for abstract thought.

The late appearance of black women as composers corresponds to a similar tardiness among white women in this country. Women composers in Europe—Hildegard von Bingen (1098–1179), Francesca Caccini (1587–1640), Elizabeth Jacquet de la Guerre (1666–1729), Fanny Mendelssohn (1805–1947) and many others—had been systematically ignored by historians in the belief that they were incapable of the creative intellect necessary to produce significant works of art. In the United States, social conventions and prejudices regarding women were also strong, and the opportunities to overcome them more scarce, so it took much longer for women composers of significant music to emerge. Although a few white women composed songs and parlor piano pieces and attempted to study music seriously, it was not until Amy Beach (1867–1944) composed her *Mass in E-flat Major, Gaelic Symphony,* and *Piano Concerto in C-sharp Minor* during the last decade of the nineteenth century that American women composers took their place alongside their male colleagues.

For that matter, white male composers in the United States were well behind their European contemporaries Hector Berlioz (1803–1869), Frederick Chopin (1810–1849), Giuseppi Verdi (1813–1901), Johannes Brahms (1833–1897), and Peter Ilyich Tchaikovsky (1840–1893), to mention just a few. The flamboyant American pianist, Louis Moreau Gottschalk (1829–1869), was one of the first composers to attempt a genuinely American style and wrote large symphonic works and operas as well as numerous piano pieces which were lightweight but effective showpieces.   The composers of the late-nineteenth-century New England School, John Knowles Paine (1839–1906) at Harvard and George Whitefield Chadwick (1854–1893) at the New England Conservatory, had studied abroad and imitated the European models. They were successful in laying the groundwork for future generations of American composers.   Edward MacDowell (1860–1908), the best-known nineteenth-century American composer, studied for ten years in Germany and composed large symphonic and chamber works as well as characteristic piano pieces in late-Romantic style.   Charles Ives (1874–1954) wrote unorthodox and distinctly American music in obscurity until he was discovered in the 1930s.

The music of black male composers of the nineteenth century, like that of women, reflected the stereotypical roles they were expected to play in society.   They had greater latitude for professional composition than women because a tradition had been established of slave musicians providing dance music.   The public was accustomed to black bandsmen for their dancing and black performers for their entertainment.   Band leaders Frank Johnson (1792–1844), Henry Williams (1813–1903), Joseph Postlewaite (1827–1889), pianist Blind Tom Bethune (1849–1909), and minstrel James Bland (1854–1911) composed social dance music, sentimental and patriotic songs, descriptive pieces, and sacred anthems.   Most of these were published as sheet music for piano because that was the most marketable form.   The piano had become the prevailing instrument, essential to well-appointed middle-class homes as well as cabarets and sporting houses.   Like the instrument for which it was written, solo piano music reflected the latest European fashions. Negro idioms were not publicly incorporated by black male composers until the late 1800s when Ernest Hogan (1865–1909), Blind John Boone (1864–1927), Scott Joplin (1868–1917), Thomas Turpin (1873–1922) and others began to introduce ragtime rhythms into the songs and dances of minstrel shows and ballrooms.

During the years 1892–1895, Antonin Dvořák, the Bohemian nationalist composer, was director of the National Conservatory of Music in New York City.   He was interested in America's indigenous music and requested one of his students, Harry T. Burleigh (1866–1949), to sing Negro spirituals to him.   This led to his well-publicized view on the development of an American national school through the use of native materials and to his own use of Negro idioms in the *New World Symphony* and other works.   Encouraged by Dvořák, Harry Burleigh, Robert Nathaniel Dett (1882–1943), and other black composers began to use black idioms in serious art music.

At that time, it was still difficult for black composers to have their art music taken seriously by the white public and critics.   A 1914 *Chicago Tribune* review by Glenn Dillard of the first annual "All

Colored Composers' Concert" in Orchestra Hall was typical: "The successful numbers, without exception, exploited the characteristic accents of Negro folk song. The unsuccessful numbers imitated the white man's music." It remained for the early twentieth century composers William Grant Still (1895-1978) and William Levi Dawson (1899-1989) joined by Florence Beatrice Price (1887–1953) to prove the ability of the Negro composer to master large European forms. The performance of Price's *Symphony in E Minor* by Frederick Stock and the Chicago Symphony Orchestra at the Chicago World's Fair in 1933 was met by unequivocal critical praise.

Florence Price was the first black woman to produce a body of work and to join the ranks of acknowledged composers, but she was by no means the first black woman to compose. The only reference to be found, so far, to an individual black woman composer before the nineteenth century is to Theodora Gaines (or Gines), a sixteenth-century Dominican minstrel living in Cuba, who was celebrated for her songs. The next traces of music by black women composers in the United States do not appear until after the Civil War, and the earliest are references to published songs for use in concert and in the home. The first composer whose name is known was Annie Pauline Pindell (ca. 1834-1901), sometimes called the "Black Nightengale," a concert singer and songwriter who gave recitals in the Far West and even in Hawaii. One of her songs, "Seek the Lodge Where the Red Men Dwell," was listed in the *Complete Catalogue of Sheet Music and Musical Works Published by the Board of Music Trade of the United States of America, 1870.*

However, many nineteenth-century middle-class black women followed white society's feminine ideals of gentility and domesticity in which music was a graceful but superficial adornment. In 1841, a monograph by William D. Wilson, *Sketches of the Higher Classes of Colored Society in Philadelphia. By a Southerner*, described the pursuit of knowledge and culture, the prominent role of music, and the well-appointed parlors complete with piano:

> It is rarely that the Visitor in the different familes where there are 2 or 3 ladies will not find one or more of them competent to perform on the pianoforte, guitar or some other appropriate musical instrument.

The stress on "appropriate" is also born out by black author James Monroe Trotter in his *Music and Some Highly Musical People* of 1878, the earliest book by anyone on American music. In this survey of the black musical activity of his time, Trotter says:

> . . . the gentler sex are only behind the other, in possessing a

knowledge of music, to that extent which has been caused by those unreasonable, unwritten, yet inexorable rules of society, that have hitherto forbidden women to do more than learn to perform upon the pianoforte and guitar, and to sing.

Toward the end of the nineteenth century, women's music began to be looked upon as a profession rather than just an adornment. In the United States, the last decade of the century saw three books in print about the accomplishments of black women which illustrate this change. They describe the range of activities in which black women excelled and gave short biographies of outstanding individuals. Two were published in 1893 by black physicians: *Women of Distinction* by Dr. Lawson A. Scruggs and *Noted Negro Women* by Dr. Monroe A. Majors (who was the father of composer Margaret Bonds). Both authors described the careers of Amelia L. Tilghman and Mrs. N. A. R. Leslie. Amelia Tilghman was born in Washington, D.C., and graduated from the Normal Department of Howard University in 1871. She had an illustrious career as a teacher and concert singer. In 1886 she became the first Negro to publish a musical magazine, *The Musical Messenger.* Although her composing is not mentioned by Scruggs or Majors, examples of her published music are in the Library of Congress and Moorland-Spingarn Research Center at Howard University. Mrs. Leslie, whose picture appears in both books, settled in 1893 in Corpus Christi, Texas, to start a musical conservatory for young ladies. She is described by Majors as "not only talented as a reader and performer of her art, but a composer of some prominence." He goes on to say:

> Hence the race, which has produced other great minds to shine forth proclaiming progress in various walks of life may feel proud of Mrs. Leslie who along with many more of her sex, is doing what she can to explode the doctrine of *inferior music* and the appellation, *musical race in the rough.* [italics his]. Much is accomplished with hard labor, and nothing without.

Unfortunately, none of Mrs. Leslie's compositions have been found, nor has music by the other composers Majors describes: May C. Reynolds Heyers, billed as "Actress, Singer, Musician, and Writer of Operas," Mrs. Mary LeMcLemare Sinclair, "among the finest musicians in Tennessee . . . a composer of songs and many notable pieces of music," and Mrs. J. E. Edwards of Washington, D.C. and Galveston, "a scholar in piano music, both a composer and a pleasing performer."

The year after the two men published their books, Mrs. N. F. Mossell joined their ranks with *The Work of the Afro-American Woman.* While she only lists composers' names, she does forthrightly name their profession: "We have in the line of musical composers, Miss Estelle Rickets (sic), Miss Bragg, Miss Tillman (sic), Mrs. Yeocum and Mrs. Ella Mossell."

Some of these names reappear in a file of Afro-American composers compiled between 1900 and 1930 by Walter Whittlesey, former Head of the Library of Congress Music Division. From it, Wayne Shirley, music specialist at the Library of Congress, has culled a list of over two dozen women composers whose works were published before 1920. Many of the works, though not all, are to be found in the Library of Congress holdings or copyright files. The earliest are songs: "Forgive" by Louise Smith ("sung with great success by Louis L. Brown of the Callender's Minstrels"), published in Washington in 1885, followed in 1886 by "Old Blandford Church" by Lucinda Bragg ("dedicated to Hon. John Mercer Langston, ex-minister to Hayti") and "You Know" by Mrs. Sam Lucas (Carrie Melvin Lucas, wife of the famous performer) in 1887. A variety of sacred and secular sentimental songs ensued.

The first piano solo to be found at the Library of Congress is Estelle Ricketts' *Rippling Spring Waltz* of 1893, to be followed by numerous similar pieces by other composers: the ubiquitous parlor music of sedate waltzes, marches, and two-steps, and sentimental paeans to motherhood and country. Some of these pieces, however, exhibit compositional skill which makes one wonder what other work might have remained in manuscript.

None of the surviving solo piano music published by black women at that time displays black idioms, although some women collaborated with their husbands in composing "coon songs" (songs in syncopated ragtime style with lyrics that reflected white American stereotypes of black Americans) for the vaudeville circuits. In the case of Mrs. Ida Larkins (two of whose collaborations with her husband John Larkins are the coon songs "The Trolley Party in the Sky"and "Miss Hazel Brown"), her solo piano piece *Wild Flowers,* composed under her name alone, is in a very conservative, lady-like style. The piano rags, which swept the country after the turn of the century, evolved through the dubious avenue of honkytonk pianos in bawdy houses and saloons. While numerous white women composed them, there were no known black women composers of ragtime piano music. The latter may have been more constrained by church, or more at pains to distance themselves from the lower-class origins of this exotic, popular craze.

So, the music for piano by black women composers begins with the aspirations for respectability of the class which could afford both a piano and an education. The first evidence of race consciousness appears in the music of Florence Price. She was able to successfully combine the "characteristic accents of Negro folk song" with her heritage of the "white man's music."   Although Price did not usually employ actual folk melodies or quotes, she deliberately sought to imbue much of her music with characteristic black idioms such as the gapped scale and the cakewalk and juba rhythms. She alluded to this in her subtitles: the third movement of her *Symphony in E Minor* is called "Juba Dance," and her *Dances in the Canebrakes* carry the inscription, "based on authentic Negro rhythms."   In a letter of 1940 concerning her third symphony, about to be performed in Michigan under Walter Poole, she states, "It is intended to be Negroid in character and expression. In it no attempt, however, has been made to project Negro music in the purely traditional manner. None of the themes are adaptations or derivations of folk songs."

Price never traveled or studied abroad, as did many of her talented contemporaries. Women composers, in general, did not join the exodus until Nadia Boulanger became influential as a teacher in France in the 1930s. One exception was Helen Eugenia Hagan (1893?–1964), born in Portsmouth, New Hampshire and educated at the Yale University School of Music, who received Yale's Sanford Fellowship in 1912 to study composition at the Schola Cantorum with Vincent d'Indy. She remained in France for two years and returned to the United States at the outbreak of World War I. For some years, she gave highly-praised piano concerts and performed her *Piano Concerto in C Minor* on several occasions, but her concert career did not gather momentum so she turned to teaching and choral directing. Another musician who gave up composing was Nora Douglas Holt (1885–1974), the first black musician to complete the master's degree at the Chicago Musical College in 1918, with a symphonic thesis composition, *Rhapsody on Negro Themes*. She became a noted music critic and radio personality, and traveled widely as a singer/ entertainer.

Nora Holt's years in Chicago as a music student, fledgling critic for the *Chicago Defender*, and co-founder in 1919 of the National Association of Negro Musicians, point up the stimulating atmosphere and historic importance of that city in attracting and producing an unusual number of black women composers. Several factors may have contributed: the high regard for learning and culture of the early Negro upper class, the large population due to black migrations from the South starting in Reconstruction days, the isolation and independence of the black community's economic and political infrastucture, the "Golden Age of Jazz" in the 1920s and the subsequent Gospel and Soul eras, the world fairs and exhibits, and the institutions of higher learning which welcomed Negro musicians from all over the country. However, Chicago was not alone in providing a richly nurturing environment for young, black female talent. When Florence Price and her family moved there in 1926 because of racial violence in her hometown, Little Rock, Arkansas, she entered an environment, typical of the black community in many cities, of supportive fellow musicians, extended families, and neighborhoods where children went with their parents from church to church for musical concerts on Sundays. Undine Smith Moore (1904–1989) tells of the universal fascination with piano study during her childhood, and the ubiquitous question directed at proud young piano students by their elders, "You playing sheet music yet?"

The Harlem Renaissance, or New Negro Movement of the 1920s and 30s, was also felt in Chicago, and Margaret Bonds (1913–1972) grew up surrounded by its influence. Her mother, Estella Bonds, was a highly respected musician and generous hostess. Writers, artists, and musicians from around the country flowed though her home and attended her Sunday afternoon musicales. Few composers were as imbued as Bonds with the defiant Harlem Renaissance spirit of Langston Hughes's poetry, although the race-conscious ideals of the New Negro Movement were also expressed in the choral and theater works of composers Eva Jessye (b. 1895) and Shirley Graham Dubois (1904–1978). Bonds was the most gifted black woman composer of her generation and a formidable pianist—the first Negro to perform as soloist with the Chicago Symphony Orchestra. She began her composition studies with Florence Price and William Dawson, and after completing her bachelor's and master's degrees at Northwestern University, she departed for New York where she continued studies at the Juilliard School of Music. She concertized and taught, collaborated with Hughes and others in musical theater, and wrote many popular songs. In the late 1960s, she moved to Los Angeles to teach and compose, and shortly after her death in April 1972, her *Credo* for baritone, chorus and orchestra was performed by the Los Angeles Symphony Orchestra under Zubin Mehta.

The Harlem Renaissance was gone by the 1940s and 1950s, although many of its ideals continued to inspire black creative artists. The Great Depression and World War II had a sobering effect on American society, which regressed from the progress made in the 1930s in recognizing and encouraging women as well as black writers, artists, and musicians. Even so, black women composers continued to be active in diverse stylistic categories. At that time, the boundaries between jazz and so-called serious music were more defined than they are today, and the prohibitions against jazz in many black churches were more strict. On the one hand, pianists Mary Lou Williams (1910–1981) and Hazel Scott (1920–1981) developed their careers during these years alongside other great jazz women composers. On the other hand, we see the "serious" composer distancing herself from these influences, studying at high-ranking U.S. conservatories and in Europe. One of the most distinguished black women composers of our century, Julia Perry (1924–1979), established her reputation in Europe during the 1950s, organizing concert series, touring as a lecturer, and conducting performances of her orchestral and operatic works. Her music incorporates the neoclassic, dissonant, contrapuntal techniques typical of international twentieth-century style, which she infused with an intense, dark lyricism.

The last few decades have seen not just a growth in variety of compositional styles and "isms," but a less rigid demarcation between them. It is not uncommon to hear European classical or even sixteenth-century techniques combined with atonality, oriental or Afro-American idioms, electronic music, and multi media. We have seen a steady increase in numbers of woman composers, Afro-Americans included, and their racial identity has become either less or more important, depending on the decade and viewpoint. Expression ranges from the African evocations of Philippa Duke Schuyler (1931–1967) to the powerful dissonant statements of Dorothy Rudd Moore (b. 1940), and from the continuity with black American choral traditions of Undine Smith Moore (1904–1989), Betty Jackson King (b. 1928), and Lena McLin (b. 1929) to the sensitive, cerebral, twelve-tone constructions of Joyce Solomon (b. 1946). It encompasses the sophisticated blend of Hispanic, Afro-Cuban and American elements in the music of Tania León (b. 1943) as well as the Balinese gamelan influences in the works of Gertrude Rivers Robinson (b. 1927).

There are no feminine or black stereotypes here. The variety of backgrounds, styles, and degrees of sophistication is striking. So is the competence, skill, and intellectual and emotional power of much of this music. Black idioms appear, blended with European classical and other techniques, in all proportions from none at all to very prominent. Almost without exception, the affirmation of racial identity is manifested, if not in idiom, then in choice of texts or titles. These qualities of confidence, variety, freedom, and expansiveness of spirit make black women's music an essential and richly rewarding part of the musical heritage of us all, and well worth the effort of locating these scores.

Sources and Abbreviations

Abdul
Abdul, Raoul. *Blacks in Classical Music: A Personal History.* New York: Dodd, Mead, 1977.

AMC
American Music Center, 30 West 26th Street, Suite 1001, New York, N.Y. 10010-2011.(212) 366-5263.

Ammer
Ammer, Christine. *Unsung: A History of Women in American Music.* Westport, CT: Greenwood Press, 1980.

Anderson
Anderson, Ruth E. *Contemporary American Composers: A Biographical Dictionary.* Boston: G. K. Hall, 1982.

ASCAP
ASCAP Biographical Dictionary of Musicians. 4th Edition. Compiled and edited by the Lynn Farnol Group. New York: American Society of Composers, Authors, and Publishers, 1980.

Block
Block, Adrienne Fried, and Carol Neuls-Bates. *Women in American Music : A Bibliography of Music and Literature.* Westport, CT: Greenwood Press, 1979.

BMRB
Black Music Research Bulletin. Chicago: Columbia College Center for Black Music Research, 1978–1990.

BMRJ
Black Music Research Journal. Chicago: Columbia College Center for Black Music Research, 1980–.

BPiM
Black Perspective in Music. Edited by Eileen Southern. Cambria Heights, New York: Foundation for Research in the Afro-American Arts, Inc., 1973–.

BrownJWJ
Brown, Rae Linda. *Music Printed and Manuscript in the James Weldon Johnson Memorial Collection of Negro Arts and Letters.* New Haven, CT: Yale University Press, 1982.

Carter   Carter, Madison. *An Annotated Catalog of Composers
                 of Afro-American Ancestry.* New York: Vintage
                 Books, 1986.
CBMR   Center for Black Music Research, database and hold-
                 ings. Columbia College, 600 South Michigan Avenue,
                 Chicago, IL 60605.(312) 663-9463.
CBMRDig   *Center for Black Music Research Digest.* Chicago:
                 Columbia College Center for Black Music Research.
ChicHS   Chicago Historical Society, Claude Barnett Collection.
                 Clark St. at North Ave. Chicago, IL 60610.(312) MI2-
                 4600.
ChicPL   Chicago Public Library, Vivian Harsh Collection.
                 Carter Woodson Branch, 9525 S. Halsted St.,
                 Chicago, IL 60628.(312) 269-2886.
Claghorn   Claghorn, Charles Eugene. *Biographical Dictionary of
                 American Composers.* West Nyack, N.Y.: Parker
                 Publishing Co., 1973.
Cohen   Cohen, Aaron I. *International Encyclopedia of Women
                 Composers.* 2d ed. 2 vols. New York: Books and Music,
                 1985.
Dannett   Dannett, Sylvia. *Profiles in Negro Womanhood,* 2 vols.
                 New York: Negro Heritage Library, 1966.
Fischer   *Our Afro-American Heritage in Music.* Edited by
                 Herman Hemmit. Chicago: Carl Fischer Music, 1987.
Green   Green, Mildred Denby. *Black Women Composers: A
                 Genesis.* Boston: Twayne Publishers, 1983.
Handy   Handy, D. Antoinette. *Black Women in American
                 Bands and Orchestras.* Metuchen, N.J.: Scarecrow
                 Press, 1981.
Hare   Hare, Maude Cuney. *Negro Musicians and their Music..*
                 1936. Reprint. Jersey City, N.J.: Da Capo Press, 1981.
Holly   Holly, Ellistine Perkins. *Biographies of Black
                 Composers and Songwriters.* Dubuque, IA: Wm. C.
                 Brown Publishers, 1990.
JWJ   James Weldon Johnson Memorial Collection. Beinecke
                 Rare Books and Manuscript Library, Yale University
                 Library, Box 1603A Yale Station, New Haven, CT
                 06520.
LC   Library of Congress Music Division holdings. Madison
                 Building, 1st St. and Independence Ave. SE.,
                 Washington, D.C. 20540.(202) 707-5504.
LCCC   Library of Congress Copyright Division Catalog.
LCWh   Library of Congress Music Division. Walter Whittlesey
                 File of Black Composers. 1900-1930. Unpublished.

Majors	Majors, Monroe A. *Noted Negro Women: Their Triumphs and Activities.* Chicago, 1893.
Meggett	Meggett, Joan M. *Keyboard Music by Women Composers.* Westport, CT: Greenwood Press, 1981.
MoorSping	Moorland-Spingarn Research Center. Howard University. Washington, D.C. 20059. (202) 806-7480.
Mossell	Mossell, Mrs. N. F. *The Work of the Afro-American Woman.* 1894. Reprint. Freeport, N.Y.: Books for Libraries Press, 1971.
NegYB	*Negro Year Book.* Edited by Monroe N. Work. Tuskegee, AL: Tuskegee Institute, 1912–1951.
Newberry	Newberry Library. Chicago Symphony Orchestra Clipping and Programs Scrapbooks. 60 W. Walton Street, Chicago, IL 60610. (312) 943-9090.
NGrDAM	*New Grove Dictionary of American Music.* Edited by Wiley Hitchcock. London: Macmillan & Co., 1986.
NYPL	New York Public Library. Performing Arts Center. 111 Amsterdam Ave. New York, N.Y. 10023 (212) 870-1647.
Patterson	Patterson, Willis. *Anthology of Art Songs by Black American Composers.* New York: E. B. Marks, 1977.
Roach	Roach, Hildred. *Black American Music: Past and Present.* 2 vols. Boston: Krieger Publishing, 1973, 1985.
Schomburg	Schomburg Center for Research in Black Culture. 515 Lenox Ave., New York, N.Y. 10037.(212) 862-4000.
Scruggs	Scruggs, Lawson. *Women of Distinction.* Raleigh, N.C., 1893.
SouBD	Southern, Eileen. *Biographical Dictionary of Afro-American and African Musicians,* 2d ed. Westport, CT: Greenwood Press, 1982.
SouMBA	———. *The Music of Black Americans: A History,* 2d ed. New York: W. W. Norton, 1983.
Southall	Southall, Geneva Handy. "In Celebration of Black Women Composers." Program notes for fourth annual "Music of Black Composers" program at Smithsonian Institute, Washington, D.C., 15 May 1988.
Spradling	*In Black and White.* 3d ed. Edited by Mary Mace Spradling. Detroit, 1980.
Tischler	Tischler, Alice. *Fifteen Black American Composers; A Bibliography of Their Works.* Detroit: Information Coordinators, 1981.
Williams	Williams, Ora B. *American Black Women in the Arts and Social Sciences,* 2d ed. Metuchen N.J.: Scarecrow Press, 1978.

A Catalog of Solo
and Ensemble Works

Composers are listed in alphabetical order, followed by their piano solo works listed alphabetically, then piano ensemble works. Selected bibliographies are provided for those composers on whom material is available.

The author has attempted to find and personally view all the listed works. Those compositions which have been located <u>and</u> seen by the author are in **bold face**. Those in plain text have not been seen for a variety of reasons: they may be in private closed collections, or problematic to obtain, or they may be cited in one or more of the sources in parentheses at the end of the entry but have not yet been located.

The order of information is: composer's last name, given name(s), maiden name or initial, date and place of birth (n.d. or n.p. if not known), education, professional experience and other brief biographical information, types of works composed, and if available, an address for obtaining the composer's music.

Works are listed by name, instrumentation, year of composition or copyright (c.), length (in pages and/or minutes), key, time signature, tempo or other indication, and brief descriptive phrases such as rondo form, flowing counterpoint, mildly dissonant, etc. Unless a publisher is listed, it can be assumed that the music is in manuscript form.

Descriptive comments are not intended to be qualitative. The author has deliberately avoided evaluations of worth, appeal, or skill.

A level of difficulty is also assigned, but should be taken cautiously. "Easy" is the level of Schumann's *Happy Farmer* or Bach's *Minuet in G*; "moderate" is equivalent to Bach's *Two-Part Invention in F Major* or Beethoven's *Für Elise*; "moderately difficult" corresponds to Debussy's *Clair de Lune* or Joplin's *Maple Leaf Rag*; "difficult" ranges from the level of Rachmaninoff's *Prelude in C-sharp Minor* to Chopin's *Revolutionary Etude* and George Walker's *Sonata no. 1*.

If not available from an address given at the end of the composer's biography, the location (where known) of an item is indicated in parentheses after the description of the piece. "Library of Congress" indicates that the work is located and can be seen in Washington, D.C. at the Music Division of the Library of Congress. If it is not still under copyright, it is possible to obtain a photocopy at 50¢ a page ($7.00 minimum, plus postage). Requests should include as much information as possible (call numbers have been given in the catalog). Allow several weeks for processing and delivery. The address is: Library of Congress, Music Division, Madison Building, Room 113, Washington, D.C. 20540.

Sources of biographical and other information are in parentheses at the end of the entry, abbreviated according to the preceding list of Sources and Abbreviations.

Aldridge, Amanda Ira (pen name, Montague Ring)

b. 10 March 1866 in Upper Norwood, London, England; d. 9 March 1956 in London. Pianist, singer, and composer. Aldridge was the daughter of the black American actor, Ira Aldridge, and a Swedish singer. Her sister, Irene Luranah, was a concert and opera singer. Amanda attended a convent school in Belgium and received her musical training at the Royal Academy of Music, studying voice with Jenny Lind and George Henschel, elocution with Madge Kendal, and harmony and counterpoint with Frederick Bridge and Francis Gladstone. She began to sing publicly at fifteen, performing Handel's "Creation Hymns" at the Crystal Palace, and became a well-known personality in Great Britain. Her concert career was ended when a severe laryngitis attack permanently injured her voice. She coached Marian Anderson, Paul Robeson, and Roland Hayes, and many other celebrated singers. She used the name Montague Ring to separate her careers as vocal coach and composer. Her compositions include art songs, suites, sambas and light orchestra and band pieces which were widely performed in England.

Solo:
> *Bagdad. Suite for Pianoforte,* c. 1929, published by Chappell & Co., London. (Copy located at Library of Congress, call number M 24 .R58 B2.)
>> I. "The Royal Guard"; 4 pp.; C Minor (modal), 2/4, "Allegretto"; "sempre staccato"; oom-pah marching-eighth bass; alternation of two themes; modulations to

G Minor and F Minor. Moderate.

II. "The Garden Beautiful"; 4 pp.; F Minor (modal), 3/4, "Andante"; evocation of languid, exotic atmosphere; sinuous, chromatic, ornamented melody; form is A B C B A; B section in F Major and C section in C Minor. Moderate.

III "Hail! Hail! O Caliph the Great"; 3 pp.; G Minor, 4/4, "Maestoso"; in ternary form; fanfare sections frame a march which gathers momentum and volume by addition of octave doubling and flourishes; L.H. octaves, R.H. double thirds. Moderately difficult.

Carnival Suite of Five Dances, c. 1924, published by Chappell & Company in London; different from Aldridge's other suites in its European, rather than African or Arabian theme: French masquerade and pantomime theater with its stock characters.   (Copies located at the Library of Congress, call number M 24 .R58 C3, and at the Schomburg Center for Research in Black Culture, 5515 Malcolm X Blvd., New York, N.Y., 10037-1801 (212) 862-4000.)

1. "Cavalcade"; 4 pp.; C Major, 2/4, "Allegro" (quarter = 80); a fanfare and march in A B A C A form; rapid, staccato parallel sixth chords. Moderately difficult.

2. "Pierrette"; 4 pp.; E-flat Major, 4/8, "Allegretto con grazia, (Tempo sempre rubato)" (eighth = 120); a feminine version of Pierrot (a clown in whitened face and loose white clothes); playful, staccato melody; oom-pah accompaniment with wide, rapid skips; form is A B A C A; section in A-flat Major. Moderately difficult.

3. "Harlequin"; 4 pp.; G major, 4/4, "Scherzando" (quarter = 120); another stock character (rogue in multi-colored clothes, carrying a wooden sword); basically ternary, with middle sections in C Major and E-flat Major; playful, skipping melody. Moderate.

4. "Columbine"; 2 pp.; E-flat Major, 3/4, "Tempo molto lento e rubato" (quarter = 66); stock female character (the saucy sweetheart); languid melody in thirds; florid cadenza in center. Moderate.

5. "Frolic"; 4 pp.; F Major, 2/4, "Allegro" (quarter = 80); "leggiero," skipping triplet melody begins simply, becoming more doubled and elaborate with each return; alternating sections in D-flat Major; octaves, large skips. Moderately difficult.

Four Moorish Pictures, c. 1927, published by Ascherberg, Hopwood and Crew, Ltd., London. (Copy located at the

Library of Congress, call number M 24 .R58 F5.)
1. "Prayer before Battle"; 3 pp.; D Minor (modal), 4/4, "Moderato"; exotic atmosphere; alternation of static, tied half note motive, and more flowing, ornamented melody. Moderate. (Published in *Black Women Composers: A Century of Piano Music* , see Appendix 1.)
2. "Dance of the Slave Girls"; 2 pp.; D Minor (modal), 3/4; "Allegretto." Moderate.
3. "Twilight Dance"; 3 pp; F Minor (modal), 3/4, "Andante con moto (dreamily)"; sinuous, double thirds and sixths. Moderately difficult.
4. "Dance of triumph"; 4 pp.; E Minor (modal), 4/4, "Moderato Pomposo"; repeated double thirds and big chords. Moderately difficult.

Mirette Serenade, c. 1934, published by Walsh, Holmes & Co. Ltd., London; 4 pp.; E-flat Major, 2/4, "Tempo di Tango"; ternary form; graceful salon piece. Moderate. (Copy located at the Center for Black Music Research, Columbia College, 600 S. Michigan Ave., Chicago, IL 60605-1996.)

Three African Dances, 1913. Orchestration by Hale Smith performed by the Black Music Repertory Ensemble and recorded at St. Louis, Missouri in October 1989 by the Center for Black Music Research; 8 min. (See Discography.)
1. "The Call of the East"
2. "Luleta's Dance"
3. "Dance of the Warriors"

Three Arabian Dances, 1919; still tracing.

Three Pictures from Syria, c. 1924, published by Metzler & Co, Ltd., London. Moderate to moderately difficult. (Copy located at Library of Congress, call number M 24 .R58 T4.)
1. "The Desert Patrol"; 4 pp.; A Minor, 4/4, "Poco Allegretto"; "Soft drum taps on each beat, throughout"; includes melody in left hand octaves. Moderately difficult.
2. "Beneath the Crescent Moon"; 2 pp; F Minor (modal), 3/4, "Moderato, languidly"; ternary form; some right hand double thirds. Moderate.
3. "The Pursuit"; 5 pp.; G Minor, 2/4, "Allegro con fuoco"; modified rondo form. Moderately difficult.

(Carter, Cohen, Holly, LCC, NegYB1917, Southall, SouBD, Schomburg)

Alston, Lettie Marie Beckon

b. 13 April 1953 in Detroit, Michigan.   Clarinetist, guitarist, organist, pianist, xylophone player, teacher and composer.   She attended Bailey Temple School of Music and Wayne State University in Michigan (B.A., 1976; M.A., 1978) where she studied composition with James Hartway and piano with Mischa Kottler. Her D.M.A. degree in composition was completed in 1983 at the University of Michigan under Leslie Bassett, William Bolcom, and Eugene Kurzt.   She also studied electronic music with George Wilson and piano with Robert Hord and Benning Dexter.   She received the Ida K. Smokler Award in 1976, the Black American Music Symposium Award at the University of Michigan in 1985, as well as several other awards.   She was commissioned to write a work, *Conquest of Jericho* (mixed chorus, narrator, string quartet and piano), for the Lyric Chamber Ensemble's 10th Anniversary, which was performed in May 1990 by the Brazeal Dennard Chorale and Lyric Chamber Ensemble.   She taught at Wayne State University and the Detroit Public Schools, and served on the faculties of Oakland University in Michigan, and Eastern Michigan University.   She has also performed as soloist and accompanist for the Detroit Board of Education and the Brazeal Dennard Chorale. She is a member of the American Music Center, International League of Women Composers, Michigan Music Teachers Association, New Music Chicago, and Society of Composers, Inc. Her compositions include orchestral, vocal, and chamber works, and encompass a variety of styles.   Many of her works are atonal without employing serial techniques.   They may be obtained through the composer at 18654 Rainbow Drive, Lathrup Village, MI 48076.

Solo:

> *Moods for Piano*, 1976, revised 1980; 13 pp., 4 min.; three sections indicated by "Allegretto (Scherzando)" (quarter = 52), "Allegro" (quarter = 100), and "Piu Mosso et Scherzando" (quarter = 138); atonal, varying meters; contemporary piano techniques include occasional tone clusters struck with palms as well as inside-piano muted strings and strumming; conventional notation, with longer pauses marked by number indicating seconds; sparse, disjunct, widely-spaced pitches, intervals, and clusters; irregular rhythmic values contrast with middle section in continuous eighths; wide and finely differentiated expressive range; third section recalls materials of the first. Moderately difficult.

Ensemble:

Effigy, oboe, piano, and percussion, 1976.

Fantasy for Piano and Orchestra, 1983; 15 min.

The Integrated Concerto, piano and orchestra, revised and performed in 1987 at Oakland University, Michigan; 8 min.;
atonal but not particularly dissonant; opens with percussion
and winds; thematic material passes to marimba, then
horns, strings and finally to the piano; the whole work in
one continuous movement is built on the same thematic material featuring falling and rising seconds, falling fourths,
and octaves; builds to a dramatic quasi-cadenza by piano.
Difficult.

Memories, violin, cello, and piano, 1981, "Dedicated to the
memory of Pearl Roberts McCullom, my beloved godmother
and first music teacher, who gave me the greatest gift in my
life, her musical knowledge."; 48 pp., 15 min.; atonal; three
movements: "Moderato con molto espressione," "Grazioso,"
and "Energico" ending "Andante"; uses variety of string and
piano techniques (sul ponticello, piano muted strings, etc.);
program notes by the composer: "Memories of Pearl's love
are expressed by one motivic idea in the first movement.
Later this theme is disguised and incorporated into another
theme representing the illness which eventually took her
life. The second movement expresses the gay and joyful
qualities of her teaching. Memories of self-control and
discipline dominate the third movement. Finally, facing
the fact that we all live to someday die, the conflict
resolves, for life must go on, as do my memories of Pearl
Roberts McCullom. The work ends in a chorale." Difficult.

Visions, marimba and piano, 1977, revised 1979, and performed
by Larry Kaptain and Lettie Beckon at University of
Michigan Symposium on Black Women Composers on 10
August 1985; 16 pp., 8 min.; atonal; interchanging, sharing
and blending of material by the two instruments; in five
short movements. Difficult.

1. "Moderato" (quarter = 88); short introduction in 2/4 leads
to 5/4 with percussive repeated rhythmic pattern by
piano.

2. "Allegretto" (quarter = 84); increased blending of materials and timbres by the two instruments.

3. "Andante" (quarter = 60); slow introduction and a fast,
playful middle section.

4."Lento" (quarter = 56); slow opening section shifts to more
dynamic and dramatic "Allegro".

     5."Moderato" (quarter = 96); returns to the 5/4 rhythmic
     motives of the first section.

(Composer, BPiM Winter 1986, Carter, Cohen, Holly)

Bailey, Mable

b. 18 June 1939 in Canton, Mississippi. Organist, teacher, and composer. She grew up in Oakland, California, where she heard the
piano for the first time at Mt. Carmel Baptist Church when she
was nine years old. She decided then that she wanted to be a
musician. She studied both piano and voice, and attended
McClymonds High School. She received a scholarship to attend
San Francisco State University and graduated in 1963 with a double
major in education and music. She first became interested in
composing during graduate study at the University of New Mexico
in Albuquerque. She continued studying composition at the College
of the Holy Names in Oakland with Sr. Theresa Agnes. Moving to
Denver, Colorado, in 1973, she studied piano with Susan Cable at
Metropolitan Community College and composition with Norman
Lockwood, Donald Keats, and David Diamond at the University of
Denver (M.M, 1983). She has taught music in the Denver Public
Schools since 1976. Many of her compositions are sacred vocal
works. Some of her other compositions are *The Valentine Vendor*
(1980) for soprano and baritone, a dramatic, whimsical set of five
songs composed in a tonal idiom, *Krazy Kuilt* (1982) for percussion
ensemble, and a *String Quartet* (1984) in which each movement is
composed in the style of a different period. Her piano pieces are
somewhat atonal. Music can be obtained through the composer, at
11181 W. 17th Ave. #2-304, Lakewood, CO 80215.

Solo:
     Dance, 1982; 2 pp., 2 min.; no key signature, 6/8, "Presto"; lilting
       and mildly dissonant, giving it a slightly sardonic twist.
       Moderate.
     Dialogue, 1986; 5 pp., 3 min. 50 sec.; no key signature, changing
       meter, "Dramatic"; linear dissonant counterpoint in two
       voices; by turns conversational and argumentative, when
       voices become doubled in octaves; closes quietly with open-
       ing phrase. Moderate.
     Prankster, 1986; 3 pp., 2 min.; no key signature, 4/4, "Presto";
       playful and whimsical with unexpected changes in pat-
       terns and dynamics; mildly dissonant.   Moderate.

(Published in *Black Women Composers; A Century of Piano Music*, see Appendix 1.)

(*Prankster* can be played alone, or the three pieces can be performed as a set, beginning with *Prankster* and ending with *Dance.*)

Ensemble:

Kind-a Blue, flute and piano, 1981; 5 pp., 4 min.; no key signature, changing meter, "With a slight swing"; dissonant linear counterpoint with long phrases; conversational, imitative exchange between flute and piano; reflective, becoming animated at times. Moderate.

(Composer)

Baiocchi, Regina A. Harris

b. 16 July 1956 in Chicago, Illinois. Author, composer, and choral conductor. She attended Roosevelt University's Chicago Musical College, (B.A. composition, 1979), Illinois Institute of Technology's Institute of Design, and New York University (Public Relations Certificate, 1991). She is a member of the American Women Composers' Midwest Chapter. She is also an author of short stories and poetry (under pen name, Ginann). She began composing at ten, receiving encouragement and stimulation from a talented, musical family, and continued at Chicago's Paul Laurence Dunbar Vocational High School where she took trumpet and French horn, and composed for band and small groups. She has composed for orchestra, chorus, voice, chamber groups, and piano. Her songs "How it Feels to be Colored Me," and "I am Not Tragically Colored," for voice, cello, and piano, (inspired by an essay by Zora Neale Hurston), were performed in Chicago (February, 1990) and Washington, D.C. (April, 1991) by Bonita Hyman, mezzo soprano, and Philip Morehead, pianist, with cellists Betsy Start (Chicago) and Elaine Mack (Washington). Her solo trumpet sonatina, *Miles per Hour*, was performed in Chicago in May 1990 by George Vosbergh, member of the Chicago Symphony Orchestra. *Foster Pet*, for treble voice, oboe, percussion and piano, completed in August 1991, was inspired by a telephone conversation with a youthful relative. Works are available through the composer at 2605 South Indiana #1407, Chicago, IL 60616.

Solo:

> *Equipoise by Intersection: Two Piano Etudes,* 1978-79, Chicago performances by Steve Hansen and Esther Hanviriyapunt; 8 pp., 5 min.; composer's comment: "studies in technical and conceptual transition between stability (standard, nineteenth-century styles) and change (innovative, contemporary styles)"; based on a row incorporating the composer's "signature notes" also found in other works: A E E-flat B-flat; rhythms reflect love of triplets and polyrhythms; E-flat Major chord at end is "tongue in cheek"; poly–rhythms in each hand; wide range; may be interpreted in either a strict, classical idiom, or more freely in jazz idiom. Difficult. (The second *Etude* is published in *Black Women Composers: A Century of Piano Music,* see Appendix 1.)

Ensemble:

> *Chasé,* sextet for flute, alto flute, oboe, B-flat clarinet, bassoon, piano, 1978; 30 min.
>
> *Chasé,* clarinet and piano, 1978 (first movement of sextet); 5 pp.; atonal, changing meter (quarter = 60); two and three-part dissonant counterpoint; complex polyrhythms, in which moments of unison as well as regular, swaying 6/8 rhythm stand out; intertwining and sharing of material by instruments; piano also has brief solos; gently lyrical. Difficult.

(Composer, CBMR Dig. Summer 88, Holly)

Blackwell, Anna Gee

b. 24 December 1928 in Springfield, Ohio. Organist, pianist, teacher, and composer. She attended Sinclair Community College and Wright State University. She has served as chairlady and director of the Springfield chapter of the National Guild of Piano Teachers. She has been employed as financial manager at Aeronautical Systems Division for 32 years. She is the composer of vocal and keyboard works.

Solo:

> *Boogie Woogie Breakdown,* 1944.
> *Ebony Waters,* 1955.

(Cohen)

Bonds, Margaret Allison

b. 3 March 1913 in Chicago, Illinois; d. 26 April 1972 in Los Angeles. Pianist, teacher, and composer. Her father was Dr. Monroe Majors, noted physician and medical researcher, and her mother was Estella Bonds, a highly-respected Chicago musician who held Sunday afternoon musicales attended by many notable musicians. Margaret began musical studies with her mother and continued piano lessons with Tom Theodore Taylor and composition study with Florence Price and William Dawson. She attended Northwestern University (B.M. 1933, M.M. 1934) and the Juilliard School, where she studied piano with Djane Herz and composition with Roy Harris, Emerson Harper, Robert Starer, and Walter Gossett. In 1932 she received a Rodman Wanamaker prize for her song, "Sea Ghost," as well as Honorable Mention for her piano piece, *A Dance in Brown*. In 1933 she became the first black soloist with the Chicago Symphony Orchestra, performing John Alden Carpenter's *Concertino*. The next year she played Florence Price's *Concerto in D Minor* with the Chicago Women's Orchestra. She founded and directed the Allied Arts Academy for a short time in the 1930s. In 1939 she moved to New York where she taught and directed music in many organizations including Stage for Youth, East Side Settlement House, and the American Theater Wing. She was married to Lawrence Richardson, a probation officer, and had one daughter, Djane, named after Djane Herz. In 1967 she moved to Los Angeles and taught at the Inner City Institute and Repertory Theater. Her *Credo* (text by W. E. B. Dubois) for baritone, chorus and orchestra was performed by the L.A. Symphony Orchestra under Zubin Mehta shortly after her death in April 1972. A prolific composer, she wrote primarily for voice, chorus, and musical theater. She collaborated with Langston Hughes on a cantata *Ballad of the Brown King*, and on *Shakespeare in Harlem*, *Romey and Julie* and other theater works. Her popular songs include "Peachtree Street," and "Spring Will Be So Sad." *Three Dream Portraits* are art songs on texts by Langston Hughes. Her arrangements of spirituals have been commissioned and sung by numerous concert artists, including Betty Allen and Leontyne Price. Some of her out-of-print published vocal works can be obtained on interlibrary loan from libraries such as the Detroit Public Library's Azalia Hackley Collection. Many of her unpublished compositions were given away and have not been located.

Solo:

> *Lillian M. Bowles First Edition of 12 Easy Lessons and Exercises For The Piano*, composed, edited and compiled by Margaret

Bonds, published by The Bowles Music House, Chicago, 1939. (out of print, located in JWJ); 22 pp.; beginning explanations, exercises, little pieces by other composers, including Anna Louise DeRamus (Bonds' student at the Allied Arts Academy).

Clandestine on the Morning Line, ca. 1961; incidental music for a stage play; performed October 1961 in New York (Tischler); still tracing.

Compositions for the Dance, ca. 1939; listed on an Allied Arts Academy concert program in JWJ; still tracing.

A Dance in Brown, 1931; received Honorable Mention in Rodman Wanamaker Competition; (Cohen, Green, Tischler, etc.); still tracing.

Improvisation on a Spiritual Theme, ca. 1939; listed on an Allied Arts Academy program in JWJ; still tracing.

A Spanish Mother, ca. 1939; listed on an Allied Arts Academy concert program in JWJ; still tracing

Three Sheep in a Pasture, c. 1940; (Tischler); still tracing.

Spiritual Suite, n.d.; (Cohen, Green, Tischler, etc.); still tracing.
1. "The Valley of the Bones" based on "Dry Bones."
2. "The Bells" based on "Peter, Go Ring dem Bells."
3. "Group Dance" based on "Wade in the Water."

Troubled Water, published in 1967 by Sam Fox Publishing Co.; recorded by Ruth Norman on Opus One, #39; composer's arrangement for orchestra in the private collection of Albert McNeil; based on the spiritual, "Wade in the Water"; 6 pp., 5 min; E Minor, 3/4, "Allegro"; in ternary form with a coda; strongly rhythmic as well as lyrical; incorporates blues and jazz idioms; sectional changes in tempi; requires large hands, agility, and co-ordination to project melody while playing inner voices with the same hand. Difficult. (Published in *Black Women Composers: A Century of Piano Music,* see Appendix 1.)

Ensemble :
I Want Jesus to Walk with Me, cello and piano; performed by Kermit Moore in Maryland on 10 September 1964 (Tischler).

The Migration, ballet for piano and ensemble; performed at YM-YWHA in New York City on 7 March 1964 (Tischler).

Quintet in F Major, for piano quintet, 1933; in one movement (Tischler).

Troubled Water, arranged by composer for cello and piano, 1964; in possession of Kermit Moore, cellist.

Selected Bibliography:

Bonds, Margaret. "A Reminiscence." In *The Negro in Art and Music* , 191–193. New York: International Library of Negro Life and History, 1968.

Green, Mildred Denby. "Margaret Bonds." Chap. 3 in *Black Women Composers: A Genesis*. Boston: Twayne Publishing, 1983.

Patterson, Willis. *Anthology of Art Songs by Black American Composers*. New York: E. B. Marks, 1977.

Tischler, Alice. "Margaret Bonds." In *Fifteen Black American Composers; A Bibliography*, 37–58. Detroit: Information Coordinators, 1981.

Yuhasz, H.J. "Black Composers and their Piano Music." *American Music Teacher* 19 (February/March 1970):24–24.

(Ammer, Anderson, ASCAP, Block, BrownJWJ, Carter, Cohen, Green, Hare, JWJ, Meggett, NegYB1952, NGrDAM, Roach, SouBD, SouMBA, Tischler, Williams, etc.)

Butler, Jean

b. (n.d.) in Cleveland, Ohio. Classical and jazz pianist, teacher, arranger, and composer. She graduated from Oberlin Conservatory of Music, where she studied with Herbert Elwell. She also studied at the Dalcroze School of Music, the University of Hawaii, and under Mark Fax at Howard University. She teaches classical and jazz piano, voice, theory and eurythmics at the Selma Levine School of Music in Washington, D.C. She has performed as a jazz pianist with Pearl Bailey, Andrew White and Johnny Hartman, and received a composer's grant from the Cafritz Foundation. Her works, which include band pieces, art songs, piano and flute works, and two-piano compositions, exhibit a variety of influences and styles, and are characterized by an emphasis on rhythm, motion, and an improvisational quality. Her works are unavailable at present, but inquiries can be directed to her at the Levine School, 1690 36th St. NW, Washington, D.C. 20007.

Ensemble:

> *Dance Suite*, 2 pianos, commissioned by the Selma Levine School, 1986-87; three movements including a "Tango" and "Hoedown."
>
> *Maria's Rags*, 2 pianos, 1985, commissioned, performed and recorded by duo-pianists Leanne Rees and Stephanie Stoyanoff (see Discography); 6 min. 9 sec.; two pieces in ragtime style (Butler's first and only works thus far in ragtime style, composed on request).

Mermaid's Aria, 2 pianos, 1991; arrangement of the aria from
Francesca Caccini's opera *La Liberazione di Ruggiero
dall'isola d'Alcina.*

(Composer, program notes for American Women Composers' Chamber
Concert , 13 April 1986 in Washington, D.C.)

Capers, Valerie Gail

b. 24 May 1935 in New York, New York. Classical and jazz pianist,
composer, arranger, and educator. She lost her sight at age six and
attended the New York Institute for the Education of the Blind.
She studied at the Juilliard School of Music in New York, completing the Bachelor of Science degree in 1959 and the Master of Science
degree in 1960. She has taught at the Manhattan School of Music
and Hunter College (New York City). She holds the rank of Full
Professor and at present serves as chairman for the Department of
Music and Art at Bronx Community College of the City University
of New York where she has been on the faculty since 1971.
Although a classical pianist, she developed a great love and en-
thusiasm for jazz. She was influenced and encouraged by her late
brother, Bobby Capers, who played flute, alto, tenor, and baritone
saxophones with Mongo Santamaria. Her father, Alvin Capers,
was a musician and played stride piano. Her recordings (both performance and compositions) began in the 1960s. She has appeared
several times at the Newport and Kool Jazz Festivals and has performed on numerous occasions on both radio and television. Among
these appearances was a performance with Dizzy Gillespie in the
"Jazz in America" series. Among the grants received by Ms. Capers
are The National Endowment for the Arts (1976), the City
University of New York Research Foundation (1983), a commission
from the New Music Consort (1985), and a commission from the
Smithsonian Institute (1987). She was selected by the *Essence
Magazine* as "Woman of Essence" in music in 1987. Her works include several vocal, instrumental and chamber compositions; among
the most popular are *Sing About Love,* a Christmas Cantata (1974),
In Praise of Freedom, a choral and instrumental work based on the
March on Washington speech of Dr. Martin Luther King, Jr., *Psalm
150,* a choral and jazz ensemble composition, and *Sojourner,* on the
life of Sojourner Truth. Her compositions are available through the
composer: Valerie Capers, 800 Grand Concourse #4DS, Bronx, New
York 10451.

Solo:

> *Portraits in Jazz,* 1976; 23 pp., 15-20 minutes; twelve pieces,
> each dedicated to a particular musician, and each with
> prefatory remarks by the composer, from which some of the
> following comments have been taken. The pieces are in-
> tended to be pedagogical in the spirit of Schumann's *Album
> for the Young,* and are meticulously fingered and marked.
> ("Blues for the Duke," "A Taste of Bass," and "Billie's
> Song," are published in *Black Women Composers: A
> Century of Piano Music,* see Appendix 1.)
> I. "Ella Scats the Little Lamb"; 1 and 1/2 pp.; F Major, 4/4
> (half note = 88), "Bright and Spirited"; L.H. walking
> bass in half-notes; R.H. melody in Ella Fitzgerald's
> improvisatory style of "scat" singing. Easy to moder-
> ate.
> II. "Waltz for Miles"; 2 pp.; G Major, 3/4 (quarter = 80),
> "Slow and Pretty - Cantabile"; simple melody paying
> tribute to Miles Davis' sensitivity of phrasing and
> warm impressionistic harmonies. Easy to moderate.
> III. "Sweet Mister Jelly Roll"; 2 pp.; C Major, 4/4,
> "Moderately (Ragtime style) - to be played with spirit
> and humor." Easy to moderate.
> IV. "The 'Monk' "; 2 pp.; G Major, 4/4, (quarter = 160);
> "Moderately - In a playful and joking manner"; written
> in keyboard style of Thelonious Monk; open fifths and
> sevenths, biting seconds, off-balance accents, cluster
> chords, with a quote from Monk's "Straight No
> Chaser." Moderate.
> V. "Blues for the 'Duke' [Traditional Blues]"; 2 pp.; F
> Major, 4/4 (quarter = 69), "Moderato (Moody)"; twelve-
> bar blues form; theme with two variations and return,
> reminiscent of early style of Duke Ellington. Easy to
> moderate.
> VI. "A Taste of Bass"; 2 pp.; C Major, 4/4 (quarter = 126)
> "Marcato with Fun and Spirit"; dedicated to bassist
> Ron Carter; first seventeen measures are a miniature
> bass solo, followed in measures 18–24 by a walking bass
> line. Easy to moderate.
> VII. "Billie's Song"; 1 p.; C Major, 4/4 (half note = 60),
> "Slow and Lyrical"; simple, one page ballad dedicated
> "in fondest memory" to Billie Holliday. Easy to mod-
> erate.
> VIII. "Mr. 'Satchmo' "; 2 pp.; C Major, 4/4 (half note = 50);
> in the style of the old New Orleans street bands; the

R.H. imitates Louis Armstrong's early trumpet playing. Easy to moderate.
IX. "Cancion de la Havana"; 2 and 1/2 pp.; E Major, 4/4, "Allegro Vivace"; improvisational in spirit, this piece combines flamenco and Western African influences. Moderate.
X. "Bossa Brasilia"; 2 pp.; C Major, 4/4 (half note = 63), "Moderato - Easy and Pretty Tempo"; flavor of the bossa nova; rhythmically tricky, with repetition of the dotted quarter and eighth note patterns in the L.H., against the off-beat quarter notes of the R.H. Moderate.
XI. "Blue-Bird [Chromatic Blues]"; 2 pp.; C Major, 4/4 (half note = 76), "Fast and Bright"; a harmonically expanded blues; extended, bebop melodic line with off-beat accents characteristic of Charlie ("Bird") Parker. Moderately difficult.
XII. "Cool-Trane"; 2 pp.; 4/4 (half note = 120); shifting tonality; a tricky piece which creates a melodic line similar to that played on the saxophone, closing with a quote from John Coltrane's "Cousin Mary." Difficult.
All of the pieces in this set would work well either separately, in small groups, or as the whole suite.

Selected Bibliography:
Palmer, Robert. "Concert: Valerie Capers." *New York Times* (20 December 1978):C21.
Wilson, John S. "Valerie Capers to Conduct Her Jazz-based Cantata." *New York Times* (16 December 1978).
———. "An Imaginative Approach." *New York Times* (2 July 1973).
———. "Jazz: By Valerie Capers." *New York Times* (28 February 1981)
(Composer, Southall, SouBD, clipping file at the NYPL Music Division, Lincoln Center, New York City)

Coleridge-Taylor, Avril Gwendolyn

b. 8 March 1903 in South Norwood, England. Pianist, conductor, and composer. She is the daughter of composer Samuel Coleridge-Taylor. Her first composition, written at age twelve, won a scholarship to study composition and piano at Trinity College of Music in 1915. She was the first woman to conduct the band of Her Majesty's Royal Marines. She also conducted the BBC and London Symphony Orchestras, among many other groups, and founded her own orchestra and chorus. Her compositions, numbering close to ninety works, include an orchestral work, *To April*, which was widely performed, and *Ceremonial March*, written to celebrate Ghana's independence in 1957, as well as several orchestral pieces, chamber works, songs, and piano pieces. Copies of the manuscripts of most of the works may be ordered from Boosey & Hawkes, 295 Regent Street, London, England, W1R 8JH. Allow several months for delivery.

Solo:
>*All Lovely Things*
>*Concert Etude*
>*Caprice (Cohen)*
>*Evening Song*
>*Four Characteristic Waltzes (Cohen)*
>*The Garden Pool*
>*Historical Episode (Cohen)*
>*In Memoriam*
>*Just as the Tide was Flowing: Berceuse and Nocturne*
>*Meditation*
>*My Garden(Cohen)*
>*Pastorale*
>*Rhapsody, Op. 174*
>*Sussex Landscape*
>*Two Short Pieces for Piano:*

Ensemble:
>*Concerto in F Minor for Piano and Orchestra*, 1936.
>*Crepuscule d'une nuit d'été*, flute and piano
>*Fantasie*, violin and piano
>*Fantaisie pastorale*, flute and piano
>*Idylle*, flute and piano
>*Impromptu in A Minor*, flute and piano
>*A Lament*, flute and piano
>*Reverie*, cello and piano
>*Romance*, violin and piano

(Boosey & Hawkes, Carter, Cohen, Handy, SouBD, Southall)

Coltrane, Alice McLeod

b. 27 August 1937 in Detroit, Michigan. Harpist, organist, pianist, percussionist, and composer. She began performing with The Terry Gibbs Quartet in the early 1960s, playing vibraphone and piano. She was married to John Coltrane, legendary jazz saxophonist, and replaced McCoy Tyner in Coltrane's group in 1966. Following his death in 1967, she continued to incorporate the ideas they had developed together, of expressing spiritual and mystical values in their music. She led her own groups, performing at the Village Vanguard and Carnegie Hall in New York City, and has recorded her own music combining African and Asian mysticism with Western sounds, including *Oh Allah, Journey in Satchidananda,* and *Blue Nile.*

Ensemble:
> *Bliss: The Eternal Now,* piano, harp and guitar
> *A Monastic Trio* (instrumentation?)

(Cohen, Handy)

Corrothers-Tucker, Rosina Harvey

b. late-nineteenth century. Composer and teacher. She composed in Washington, D.C. as early as 1902, when her *Rio Grande Waltzes* were published by E. F. Droop in Washington, D.C. She is listed in the Washington City Directory from 1915 as Rosina Carrothers (sic) living on 20th St. NW, then Girard St. NW until 1923, when she is listed as Rosene C. Tucker; then Rosina C. Tucker, music teacher, at 1128 7th St. NE. She is still listed under that name and address in 1940 as "Sec. treas., Ladies Aux. Brotherhood of Sleeping Car Porters," and finally, in 1969, she is listed as "Rosina C. Tucker, retired." In 1939, a song, "Marching Together" was copyrighted and published by her, dedicated to the Ladies Auxiliary of the Brotherhood of Sleeping Car Porters. I am indebted to Bonnie Hedges for this information and for the compositions, which may be requested from Dr. Hedges at The Historical Society of Washington, D.C., 1307 New Hampshire Ave. N.W., Washington, D.C. 20036 (202) 785-2068

Solo:
> *The Rio Grande Waltzes,* c. 1902, "published for the author [Rosina Harvey] by E. F. Droop & Sons"; 5 pp.; G Major; a long (sixteen measures plus repeats) introductory page in 6/8 leads to the first of three waltzes; the last two have their own introductions, and each is in binary form in eight- or sixteen-measure sections with second endings; features considerable ornamentation, chromatic passing tones, R.H. octave passage-work, and wide L.H. skips in the accompaniment; the whole is rounded off with a return to the first

waltz and a grand finale in octaves. **Moderately difficult.**
Untitled manuscript by Rosina Corrothers, n.d.; 1 p.; G Major,
3/4, "Tempo di Valse"; form is A B C A (da capo al fine),
each section sixteen measures in length with second endings;
legato, three-note falling phrases in section A become stac-
cato, three-note rising phrases in section B; graceful, lilting
waltz. Easy.

(Bonnie Hedges)

Donegan, Dorothy

b. 6 April 1926 in Chicago, Illinois. Pianist, organist, and composer.
She began piano study at five, and attended the Chicago public
schools. At DuSable High School, her music teacher was the
legendary Walter Henri Dyett. She studied piano with Rudolph
Ganz at the Chicago Musical College and later attended the
University of Southern California. She made her debut as a classical pianist at Orchestra Hall in Chicago in 1942, and continued to
perform the classical repertory, including an appearance as soloist
in the Grieg *Piano Concerto* with the New Orleans Philharmonic
at Tulane University in 1976. She was a church organist from an
early age and began playing jazz piano at age seventeen with The
Bob Tinsley Band, developing a flamboyant stage style. She
appeared in the motion picture *Sensations of 1945* and in the
Broadway musical *Star Time* (1945) and made a number of recordings. Her Dorothy Donegan Trio appeared at the Newport Jazz
Festival at Carnegie Hall in New York. In 1978, Chicago Mayor
Michael Bilandic proclaimed her birthday "Dorothy Donegan Day
in Chicago."

Solo:
> *Dorothy Donegan's Musical Compositions,* published in 1954;
> (SouBD); still tracing.
> *Modern Piano Transcriptions,* c. 1945 by publisher, Robbins
> Music Corp., New York; jazz versions of classics. **All mod-**
> **erately difficult.** (Copy at the Library of Congress, call
> number M32.8 D66M6.)
>> *Hungarian Dance no. 5;* 6 pp.; **F-sharp Minor, 2/4,**
>> **"Moderato"**; Johannes Brahms's *Hungarian Dance* first
>> presented in "straight" form; a change to "Fast Swing
>> Tempo" in cut time, and theme is varied in a free fan-
>> tasy; shifts to G Minor, D Major.
>> *Minute Waltz;* 6 pp.; **D-flat Major, 3/4, "Molto vivace";**

opens with 1 and 1/2 pages of Chopin's *Waltz;* changes to "Fast fox trot," cut time and an eleven-measure introduction with broken-octave tremolo in L.H.; the melodic motives of the waltz are adapted to duple time with a stride bass; passages of boogie woogie L.H. octave ostinato against punctuating R.H. tenth chords.

Dark Eyes; 4 pp.; D Minor, 2/2, "Moderato"; A. Salami's theme is introduced with five measures of "rubato" chords; change to "Medium swing tempo" and syncopated chords with a walking bass in tenths; then to "Fast swing tempo" and more variations upon the chromatic motive of the melody.

Liebestraum; 6 pp.; A-flat Major, 6/4, "Poco allegro con affetto"; a one page introduction of the "straight" version of Franz Liszt's piece, followed by a syncopated version, "Medium swing tempo," with stride bass, in C Major, then A-flat major.

Prelude in C-sharp Minor; 5 pp.; C-sharp Minor, 4/4, "Lento"; Rachmanininoff's *Prelude* for one page; then "Fast fox trot" and cut time, with a motoric, continuous R.H. in eighth-notes noodling the chromatic intervals of his theme against a broad, half-note walking bass, also incorporating intervals of the theme; finishes with a flashy chromatic run in octaves, alternating hands.

(Handy, SouBD)

Edwards, Mrs. J. E.

b. late-nineteenth century. Pianist and composer. She was the adopted daughter of the Right Reverend Richard Cain, D.D., of Washington, D.C. She moved to Galveston and was known as a "pleasing performer" and a composer of piano music. None has been located so far.

(Majors)

Eubanks, Rachel Amelia

b. (n.d.) in San Jose, California. Administrator, educator, and composer. She received the B.A. degree from the University of California in 1945, an M.A. from Columbia University, New York

City in 1947, and the D.M.A. from Pacific Western University in California in 1980. She also attended the Eastman School of Music, the University of Southern California, and the Westminster Choir College. In the summer of 1977, she studied with Nadia Boulanger at the American Conservatory at Fontainebleau, France. She was a Mosenthal Fellow at Columbia University in 1946 and received a Composition Award from the National Association of Negro Musicians in 1948. She is a member of Alpha Mu Honor Society, Music Educators National Conference, National Association of Music Teachers and the Society of Ethnomusicology. She has written a text book, *Musicianship*, Vols. 1 and 2. Her compositions include a *Cantata for Chorus and Orchestra* (1947), a *Symphonic Requiem* for orchestra and four solo voices (1980), and a chamber work, *Our God* (n.d.) for seven instruments and solo voice on a text by Kahlil Gibran. Inquiries may be directed to the composer at her address: 4928 Crenshaw Blvd., Los Angeles, California 90043.

Solo:
> *Interludes for Piano*, 1984; 12 pp.; five pieces: atonal, contrapuntal, concentrated (similar intervallic cells in all five), introverted.   Moderately difficult.
>> 1. "Moderato"; 1 p.; 6/8, (eighth = 132); quartal harmonies; gently dissonant; intervals more wide and open than subsequent *Interludes;* legato, expressive, pensive.
>> 2. "Moderato"; 1 and 1/2 pp.; begins and ends in F tonality, changing meters, (eighth = 112); whole and half steps dominate texture, both vertical and horizontal; mysterious, concentrated.
>> 3. "Moderato"; 3 pp.; atonal, changing meters, (quarter = 63); opens and closes with tentative, fragmentary three-note motives composed of minor second and major or minor third; motive taken up in restless, convoluted sixteenth note figuration; octave displacements; sixteenths build, hands together, to *ff* before subsiding and closing tentatively as it began.
>> 4. "Larghetto"; 3 pp.; changing meters, (quarter = 66); similar intervallic cells to third *Interlude;* wide dynamic contrast; forceful.
>> 5. "Larghetto"; 3 pp.; changing meters, (quarter = 56); a broad, long-breathed R.H. melody over a wide-ranging sixteenth note L.H. accompaniment which meanders dreamily; R.H. shifts to oscillating triplet eighths before quiet, mysterious close.
> *Prelude for Piano*, published in 1940 by Music Mart in Oakland

California; 3 pp.; E Major/ C-sharp Minor, 4/4, "Moderato"; tonal, straightforward; chordal sections frame a contrapuntal section and a bell-like, broken octave (R.H.) passage marked "Adagio." Moderate. (Library of Congress, call number M25.E.)

Ensemble:

> *Trio* for clarinet, violin, and piano, 1977; 36 pp., 25 min.; three movements; atonal; unusual massive textures. Difficult.
>
> > I. "Adagio con espressione"; changing meters (quarter = 54); begins sparsely and quietly, introducing motives gradually, the instruments alternating; melodies then develop and build, the texture becoming more continuous and thick as instruments play simultaneously and piano part adds figuration, piling up blocks of sonorities.
> >
> > II. "Allegro"; 6/8, Dorian mode, (dotted quarter = 116); opens with continuous-eighth accompaniment pattern, R. and L.H. together in contrary-motion; medieval, dance-like, jingly melody with repeated motives; five-part form A B A C A with alternating sections in simple meters and slower tempi; each return of A varies figuration and texture; bright, open sound.
> >
> > III. "Lento"; changing meters, (quarter = 50); the spiritual-like theme which opens in a call and response between piano and the other two instruments dominates and unifies this movement, becoming altered and appearing in 5/4, 6/4, 4/4 meters with varying counterpoints; when the three instruments state it in imitation, mixed (poly-) meters are employed to retain individual downbeats; massive layers of shimmering sound are piled up by piano octave doubling and figuration as well as violin double, triple, and quadruple stops; it thins and subsides to a quiet close.

(Composer, Carter, Roach, *International Who's Who in Music* 1989)

Forster, Estelle Ancrum

b. 1887 in Wilmington, North Carolina. She composed a musical play published by Theodore Presser, and some piano compositions. None have been located so far.

(Roach)

Gillum, Ruth Helen

b. 1909(?) in St. Louis, Missouri. Pianist, educator, arranger, and composer. Gillum was educated at the New England Conservatory of Music in Boston, Boston University, Prairie View College in Texas, and the University of Kansas, where she completed her B. Mus. and M. Mus. Her 1943 master's thesis was titled "Influences of the Negro Folk Song in American Music." She was employed at the radio station WREN in Lawrence, Kansas in the early 1930s and taught at Philander Smith College, Arkansas, and North Carolina College in Durham (1944).   Two of her choral spiritual arrangements are at the Library of Congress: *Roll Jordan Roll* (1937) and *There's No Hiding Place* (1948). She is also reported to have composed piano works published by J. Fischer, but none have been located so far.

(Carter, LCC, Roach, Spradling)

Goodwin, Anna Gardner

b. late-nineteenth century. Composer. Her name appears in the Walter Whittlesey File of Black Musicians at the Library of Congress. Her provenance is deduced from the dates and places of the published compositions which can be found at the Library of Congress. They include, besides the piano works listed below, a song "Adelene" published by the composer in Augusta, GA, in 1909. She may be the same Anna G. Goodwin listed in the 1900 U.S. Census Reports as black, born October 1874 in Georgia, wife of clergyman George Goodwin and mother of four-year-old George Jr., residing at 1319 Mange Street in Augusta, Georgia.

Solo:

> *Cuba Libre. Cuban Liberty March,* copyrighted in 1897 and published by the composer in Augusta, Georgia; 3 pp.; E flat major/A flat Major, 4/4; five sections, A B C D E Fb, with a four-measure introduction and some unusual transitions; most sections are eight measures long with repeat; technically more demanding (L.H. skips, R.H. double sixths) than the usual parlor music; changes of key; a variety of figuration and changes of pace and mood. Moderately difficult. (Published in *Black Women Composers: A Century of Piano Music,* see Appendix 1.)
> *The Educational Congress March,* "for Pianoforte", copyrighted in August, 1902 and published in Atlanta, GA. by the com-

poser to commemorate a Negro Young Peoples' Christian and Educational Congress held in Atlanta in August 1902; 3 pp.; F Major/B flat Major; 6/8 "Con Spirito"; four sections, A B C C^1 with a four-measure introduction and eight-measure transition between C and C^1 sections are either sixteen measures repeated with second ending, or thirty-two measures, written out; octaves, large L.H. leaps in accompaniment. Moderately difficult.

(LCWh, also Wayne Shirley, Music Librarian at the Library of Congress)

Gotay, Frances (Sister Marie Seraphine)

b. 21 May 1865 in Puerto Rico; d. 11 September 1932 in New Orleans. Composer and teacher. She came to New Orleans from Puerto Rico in 1883 and joined the Roman Catholic order of the Sisters of the Holy Family. Under her religious name, Sister Marie Seraphine, she attended a Catholic music school where she learned to play many instruments. She was placed in charge of musical instruction in schools of the order, and served in that capacity for almost fifty years. Her considerable output of musical compositions has been lost, and only this one piece survives.

Solo:
La Puertorriqueña. Reverie, published in 1896 by Junius Hart in New Orleans, dedicated "In memory of the late Rev. Mother Magdalene of the Sisters of the Holy Family"; 4 pp.; A-flat Major, 6/8, "Allegretto"; theme and variation form; a four-measure introduction leads into a "Tema" marked "espressivo" with melody in octaves over an arpeggiated accompaniment; seven variations: R.H. broken octave figuration, rapid repeated notes, rolled chords, arpeggiation, trills, melody switched to L.H., and concluding with a "Marche Royal". Moderately difficult. (Copy at the Marcus Christian Collection, Archives and Manuscripts/ Special Collections, Earl K. Long Library, University of New Orleans, Lakefront, New Orleans, LA 70148.)

(Southall, Lester Sullivan, "Composers of Color of Nineteenth-Century New Orleans: The History Behind the Music." Black Music Research Journal 8, no. 1 (1988): 72–73.)

Greene, Diana R.

b. n.d., n.p. Pianist, music copyist, and composer. She completed her B. M. in composition at Baylor University, Waco, Texas, in 1978 and studied composition with Lukas Foss from 1978 to 1980. She has held positions as administrative assistant at the Lincoln Center Institute in New York City (1979-1981), assistant to Lukas Foss (1981-1982), program director for Chamber Music America (New York City), and music copyist for such clients as Belwin Mills, Manhattan School of Music, jazz composer Leroy Jenkins, Lukas Foss, and George Crumb. In 1984 she gave workshops on music notation and printing, music copying, and contemporary music at the El Paso Arts Festival sponsored by the El Paso Community College. Her composition, *Sohomá*, for soprano, French horn, and marimba received its first performance on the Brooklyn Philharmonic's "Meet the Moderns" series in 1983. *Cognition* for alto flute, string quartet, and percussion was premiered in Erie, Pennsylvania, in 1981 and also performed by the Longar-Ebony Ensemble at the Harlem School of the Arts in 1983. Other works are *Just a Song for Seven*, for flute, clarinet, oboe, viola, cello, bass, timpani, *Rigorisms I* for marimba (low A), *Temps* for cello, drums, and *Violets, Tiaras, Braided Rosebuds* for soprano and oboe. A few of her compositions can be borrowed from the American Music Center, 30 West 26th Street, Suite 1001, New York, N.Y. 10010-2011 (212) 366-5263.

Solo:
> *5 on 2*, 1984, performed by Max Lifchitz at the American Women Composers Festival in Boston, Massachusetts, in June 1984.

Ensemble:
> *Rigorisms II*, flute, trumpet, piano, bass, completed December 1982 and dedicated "To Betty Lou Spence, whose patronage enabled me to complete this work"; 21 pp., 6 min.; composer's note: "*Rigorisms II* is the second in a series of my 'athletic' works. The first is a strenuous piece for marimba solo written for and premiered in Kingston, Jamaica by Alan Zimmerman. Both works reflect a predilection for the energetic and precise."; (quarter = 112, "with panache throughout except for mm. 22–34's lapse into austerity." Difficult. (AMC call number M422 G7996 R5 no. 2.)
>
> *Tragedies (Trauerspiele)*, piano, oboe, and cello, completed March 1980 in New York City; "Lento, mesto." Difficult. (AMC call number M322 G7996 T7.)
>
> *Trilogy*, clarinet, violin, cello, and piano, 1984.

> *Trio*, clarinet, cello, piano, performed at the El Paso Arts
> Festival, El Paso Community College, April 1984, with the
> composer at the piano; 7 min.

(AMC)

Hagan, Helen Eugenia

b. 10 January 1893 in Portsmouth, N.H. (or, b. 1895 in New Haven
CT); d. 6 March 1964 in New York City. Pianist, teacher, and composer. She grew up in New Haven, CT, becoming organist at the
Dixwell Congregational Church at age nine. She attended the
Yale University School of Music from 1906 until 1912, studying piano with H. Stanley Knight and music history, orchestration, conducting and composition with Horatio Parker. In 1910 she received
the Certificate of Proficiency in Theory, and the following year she
was awarded the Julia Abigail Lockwood Scholarship for the best
examination in pianoforte. In 1912 she completed her B. Mus. degree, and received the high honor of a Samuel Simonds Sanford
Fellowship for two years' study in Paris at the Schola Cantorum
with Vincent d'Indy. Upon her graduation, she performed her
Concerto in C Minor with the New Haven Symphony Orchestra.
She played for U.S. Negro troops in France during World War I and
had a brief, brilliant career as a concert pianist before turning to
teaching. She earned Bachelor's degrees from Georgia State
College for Women and the George Peabody College for Teachers
where she subsequently became head of the music department. She
also taught at Bishop College in Dallas, Texas, and maintained a
studio in Morristown, New Jersey, where her husband, Dr. John
Williams, practiced medicine. In her later years she was active in
music at New York City's Grace Congregational Church.

Solo:
   "numerous compositions"; unlocated.

Ensemble:
   Concerto in C Minor, survives in an arrangement for two pianos,
      1912; 40 pp., 15 min.; in one movement; C Minor, 4/4,
      "Maestoso"; earliest extant work for piano and orchestra in
      a large form by black woman composer; in heroic, late-
      romantic style of Liszt or Rachmaninoff; form is classic
      concerto-ritornello: A B A C A B A; virtuoso, bravura piano
      part; orchestra provides introduction, interludes, accompa-
      niment, some counterpoint, and occasional dialogue with

piano; majestic opening theme by orchestra interrupted by bravura gesture from piano, which then states the opening theme with florid interpolations; piano's contrasting lyrical theme in E-flat Major returns in C Major in recapitulation; central development section in E major; last statement of main theme and bravura ending in C Major. Difficult.   (Copies of manuscript available from the Yale University Music Library, P.O. Box 5469 Yale Station, New Haven, CT 06520-5469.)

Sonatas for Violin and Piano, pre-1912; unlocated.

Selected Bibliography:

Dannett, Sylvia. *Profiles of Negro Womanhood*, Vol. 2., 139–143. New York: Negro Heritage Library, 1966.
Hare, Maude Cuney. *Negro Musicians and their Music*. 1936. Reprint. Jersey City, N.J.: Da Capo Press, 1981.

(Carter, Cohen, Hare, NegYB 1947, SouBD, SouMBA, Yale University Music Library, Hagan's correspondence with the Yale University registrar, and her transcripts, etc.)

Hairston, Jacqueline Butler

b. 18 December 1938 in Charlotte, North Carolina. Vocal coach, pianist, arranger, and composer. While in her teens, she attended the Juilliard School of Music Preparatory Division in New York City for three years. She received her B.M.E. degree from Howard University in Washington, D.C. and her M.A. degree from Teachers College Columbia University, New York City. She worked in public school music for several years before becoming assistant professor of music at the Johnson C. Smith University in Charlotte. In 1973, she moved to California where she served in the music department of the Peralta Community College District until 1988. She currently teaches voice at Laney College, and a course in Music for Young Children, at Merritt College, both in Oakland. She is Minister of Music at The Church By The Side Of The Road in Berkeley. She also coaches voice privately, performs as a solo pianist in San Francisco, and travels widely conducting choral workshops. She has made vocal arrangements of spirituals for performing artists including Helen Dilworth, Susheel Bibbs, Florence Quivar, Alpha Brawner-Floyd, William Brown, and Gregory Hopkins. Some of her works have been recorded, including *A Change Has Got to Come*, performed by the London Philharmonic with William Brown, tenor and Congresswoman Barbara Jordan narrator (Columbia Records), "Loving You" (popular song) on *Andre*

Kostelanetz Plays Superman and other Hits (Columbia Records) and *Satire* (piano and orchestra) performed by Barbara Carroll pianist (United Artists). Her *Spirituals and Songs of Jackie Hairston* is due to be published in the near future. Recent works include a song cycle, *On Consciousness Streams*, dedicated to Dr. Howard Thurman. In progress are books of children's songs and of piano pieces for beginners based on traditional African-American melodies. Inquiries about her compositions may be directed to the composer at 1200 Lakeshore Ave. #4-D, Oakland, California 94606.

Ensemble:
> *Theme and Variations on "In That Great Getting-Up Morning,"* two pianos, 1991, composed for duo pianists Delphine and Romaine; 18 pp., 7 min. Moderately difficult.
> *Satire*, piano and orchestra, performed and recorded by Barbara Carroll (see Discography).

(Composer, Roach)

Harding, Mable E.

b. around 1888 in South McAlester, Indian Territory (now Oklahoma). Composer. She attended Western University at Quindaro, Kansas, where she studied with Robert G. Jackson, and won the Inter-State Literary Society Music Composition Contest Prize in 1906. with this piano solo.

Solo:
> **Farewell Alma Mater, copyright 1907 by Albert Ross and Robert Jackson, photo of composer on cover; 4 pp.; C Minor, 3/4; consisting of an introduction and four sections, A B C A[1]; the first section is in large rolled chords, *ff*, "bravura"; the B section in E-flat Major is a melody in the bass clef with "answering" phrases in treble clef, first *pp*, then repeated an octave higher, *ff*; the C section is another new melody, "dolce," ornamented with double grace notes; the A section returns "con bravura," before concluding with an "Andante-sostenuto" coda in which the A melody is played two octaves lower in single R.H. notes while the L.H. accompaniment crosses over. Moderately difficult. (Copy available through Library of Congress, call number M25.H.)**

(LC, Moor-Spring)

Harris, Ethel Ramos

b. 18 August 1908 in Newport, Rhode Island. Pianist and composer. She studied at the New England Conservatory, Carnegie Mellon University, and Tanglewood. She won the Harvey Gaul and American Palestine Committee Scholarships, as well as Delta Sigma Theta, National Association of Negro Women and Martin Luther King, Jr. awards, and was a pianist with the National Negro Opera Company. She composed a number of songs and choral works.

Solo:

> *Paquita Mia*, published by Volkwein Bros, Inc. in 1942; still tracing.
> *Yolanda*, published by Volkwein Bros, Inc., 1942; still tracing.

(Anderson, ASCAP 1966, Carter, Cohen)

Harris, Margaret R.

b. 15 September 1943 in Chicago, Illinois. Pianist, conductor, teacher and composer. She was a child prodigy, playing in public at age three and performing a Mozart Concerto with the Chicago Symphony Orchestra at age ten. That year, she entered the Curtis Institute of Music. She continued her education at the Juilliard School of Music where she received her B.S. in 1964 and her M.S, *summa cum laude* in 1965. She taught at the Dorothy Maynor School in New York City (subsequently the Harlem School of the Arts) and made her Town Hall debut as a pianist in 1970, including her own compositions, *Myriad,* and *Collage One.* In 1971, she made her conducting debut with the Chicago Symphony Orchestra in its Grant Park Concert Series, and she has continued to be active as a conductor, conducting sixteen major American symphony orchestras to date. She also directed the Negro Ensemble Company in New York City, the New York Shakespeare Festival Company and the musicals *Two Gentlemen of Verona, Raisin, Guys and Dolls, Amen Corner,* and *Hair.* She was a co-founder of Opera Ebony and has served as panelist for The National Endowment for the Arts, National Opera Institute and Affiliate Artists. She received a National Association of Negro Musicians Award in 1972 and in 1987 she became a Dame of Honour and Merit, Order of St. John, Knights of Malta. She is a member of the American Federation of Musicians Local 802, Broadcast Music, Inc., the Juilliard Alumni Association, the National Association of Negro Musicians, the National

Association of Female Executives and Mu Phi Epsilon Sorority, and is listed in numerous references. Among her compositions are concerti, songs, instrumental pieces, and works for chorus, including *Sing Ye the Praises of the Lord.* She collaborated with Ruby Dee on the musical, *John Boscoe,* and also composed a ballet, *Goliath.* Her piano music is unavailable. Inquiries about her other works may be directed to her: 165 West End Ave. #28N, New York, N.Y. 10023.

Solo:
> *Collage One,* 1970; 17 pp. (Copy located at the Center for Black Music Research, Columbia College, Chicago).
> *Israel Suite,* 1990–91; 20 min.
> *Myriad*
> *Vineyard Suite,* 1991; 10 min.

Ensemble:
> *Concerto no. 1 for Piano and Orchestra ("North Sea Suite")*
> *Concerto no. 2 for Piano and Orchestra.*

(Carter, Cohen, CBMR, Handy, SouBD, etc.)

Harvey, Rosina, see Corrothers-Tucker, Rosina Harvey

Herbison, Jeraldine Saunders

b. 9 January 1941 in Richmond, Virginia. Violinist, educator, conductor, and composer. She graduated as salutatorian of her class from Armstrong High School in Richmond, Virginia. In 1963, she completed her B.S. degree from Virginia State College, Petersburg, Virginia, where she studied composition with Undine Smith Moore. She attended the University of Michigan at Interlochen in the summers of 1973 and 1979 studying theory and composition with George Wilson, Tom Clark and Sara Boge. She spent other summers at the University of Alaska (1985) and Central Connecticut State University (1987). In the winter of 1990 she was a student at Hampton Institute, Virginia. Her violin teachers have been Dr. Thomas C. Bridge, Percy Kalt, Walter Suede and Raymond Montoni, and she studied voice with Willis Patterson, and cello with James Herbison. In 1963 she began teaching and directing ensembles in the secondary schools in Maryland, North Carolina, and Virginia, and has been orchestra director at Dozier Middle School in Newport News, Virginia, since 1980. She has performed as violinist with the Peninsula Symphony, the Norfolk Chamber Orchestra, the Williamsburg Symphony, the Hampton University Community Orchestra, the Richmond Symphony, the University of Alaska Symphony, the Hico String Quartet, and the Newport News Orchestra Faculty Ensemble. Her memberships include the American Association of University Women, Music Educators National Conference, Tidewater Composers Guild, and the A K A Sorority. She is the wife of cellist James Herbison and mother of a son, Brian Christopher. Her works are frequently heard on radio and college programs: *Six Duos for Violin and Cello* (1976) was broadcast on WAVY Channel 10 in Virginia in 1978; *Promenade for Chamber Orchestra* was performed by the Tidewater Composers' Guild Orchestra in 1982; and the *Narrative for Voice and Orchestra, "Ain't I a Woman"* in honor of Sojourner Truth, was performed by Muriel Smith and the Richmond Chamber Players at Hampton University in 1984. *Sonata no. 1 for Unaccompanied Cello* (1978), was performed by James Herbison at the Kennedy Center in Washington, D.C. in 1980 together with *Intermezzo*, Op. 9 and the *Fantasy in Three Moods*, Op. 7, with pianist Lee Anders, and was broadcast on Channel 5. In 1990, her *Five Art Songs* were performed by Janis Rosena Peri at the National Congress of Women in Music at New York University. Her compositions include works for orchestra as well as chamber and vocal music. They are basically tonal and traditional in style, characterized by independent contrapuntal lines as well as frequent doubling at the octave. They use modal, whole-tone, diatonic and chromatic scales, frequent modulations, and mildly dissonant as well as firmly tonal harmonies. Her compositions can be obtained from the composer: Jeraldine Saunders Herbison, 114 O'Canoe Place, Hampton, Virginia 23661.

Solo:
>   *Sonata no. 1 for Piano* (formerly *Prelude and Rondo*), Op. 19, no. 2, 1981, two additional movements, 1990; 15 min.; straightforward, tonal. Moderately difficult.
>   1. "Prelude"; 3 pp., 3 min.; F Major, 3/4, "Andante Mosso et Sostenuto"; lyrical melody and simple harmonization, reminiscent of Scottish folk song; to be played expressively with rubato.
>   2. "Rondo"; 8 pp., 4 min.; D Minor, 2/4, "Allegro"; opens with fiery broken octaves in alternating hands on D, returning as rondo refrain; contrasting episodes ; coda.
>   3. "Air," 1990; 6 pp., 3 min.; E Minor, 2/4 (changing,) "Allegretto" (quarter = 85); light, graceful melody; two-part imitative counterpoint.

4. "Scherzo," 1990; 22 pp., 5 min.; A Minor, 4/4, "Allegro" (quarter = 96); fiery chromatic scales, octaves, rhythmic repeated chords. Technically more difficult.

Ensemble:

An Invention Upon an Airy Upland, Op. 24, cello and piano, 1990; commissioned and performed by James Herbison, cellist; 22 pp., 6 min.; D Major, 3/4, "Largo cantabile"; melody inspired by poem of George Russell: "Upon an airy upland within me and far away, a child who ageless dances . . ."; cello begins alone with lilting melody; first four sixteenth-notes taken up by piano and expanded; figuration suggests Baroque music; a brief passage in "chorale style"; modulates to other keys, ending firmly in C Major. Moderately difficult.

Fantasy in Three Moods, Op. 7, cello or viola and piano, 1971; has received numerous performances; 10 pp., 7 min.; lyrical, impressionistic work with some jazz harmonies; shifting tonalities; mildly dissonant. Moderately difficult.

1. "Jovial"; 3/4, "Allegretto"; airy and cheerful; alternating sections of 3/4 and 4/4.
2. "Pensive"; starts 5/4, "Lento"; more moody and tempestuous; free rhythmic structure; begins and ends with same four notes chosen by the composer "when strumming an out-of-tune guitar."
3. "Vacillation"; 2/4, "Allegro con brio, et Larghetto"; lively rhythmic sections alternate with moody, gruff passages.

I Heard the Trailing Garments of the Night, Op. 10, flute, violin, cello, and piano, 1975; began as an art song on H. W. Longfellow's poem and changed to a quartet; 14 pp., 6 min.; D minor tonality, changing meters; opens with a free, unmetered, solo violin cadenza (written out), followed by a solo cello cadenza beginning with the same five-note motive as the violin; the flute enters at "Allegretto" with a new theme accompanied by piano arpeggiation in triplets; interchanging of thematic material; a section of staccato, pizzicato, and ponticello; both string and flute themes recalled before close. Moderately difficult.

Intermezzo, Op. 9, cello and piano, 1978, revised and arranged from a 1969 piece for violin and piano; 6 pp., 3 min.; G major, 4/4, "Andante con moto"; graceful, lyrical melody with traditional tonal harmonies; three sections and coda; third section more aggressive; coda brings back thematic material from the first section. Moderate.

Introspection, Op. 8, flute, violin, cello, piano, 1973; 4 pp., 5 min.; atonal, changing meters, "Andante"; experiment in twentieth-century techniques; two different "Andante" sections followed by "Allegretto agitato," then return of theme from first section. Moderately difficult.

Metamorphosis, 2 violins, cello, guitar, piano, 1978; memorial piece for deceased mother; 7 pp., 5 min.; C Minor (ends in major), changing meters, "Largo" (quarter = 54); elegiac; primarily tonal with atonal passages; unusual timbres (guitar sound creates a timbral bridge between strings and piano). Moderately difficult.

Miniature Trio, Op. 3, oboe, violin and piano, 1962, revised and absorbed into *Suite no. 3* for chamber orchestra, oboe and flute.

Nocturne, oboe, violin and piano, 1961, also absorbed into *Suite no. 3.*

Piano Quartet, Op. 18, no. 1 (*Melancholy on the Advent of Departure*), 1980, commissioned by the Williamsburg Chamber Players; 10 min.; similar to *Introspection* and *I Heard the Trailing Garments of the Night:* experiments with twentieth-century atonal techniques.

Sonata no. 2 for Cello and Piano, Op. 19 no.1, 1981; numerous performances by James Herbison, cellist; 30 pp., 15 min.; basically tonal, mildly dissonant; two movements in rounded binary form. Difficult.

   I. "Adagio"; changing meters (quarter = 60); dramatic, rhapsodic; begins with long, lyrical cello solo; piano enters with counter theme, crystalline figuration in high register.

   II. "Allegro"; 2/4; energetic, lively; dialogue between cello and piano; theme of first movement returns, its character transformed with different piano part; mysterious, passionate; movement ends with cello solo.

Trio no. 3 for Violin, Cello, and Piano, Op. 22, no. 2, 1986, commissioned and performed by Nova Trio, at Old Dominion University, the Chrysler Museum, and the Wells Theater with the Tidewater Ballet Company; 33 pp., 20 min.; tonal; traditional harmonies freely combined with non-traditional; composer "aspired to represent the soul of innocence, youth, naiveté, minorities, . . . crushed by tribulations of life, yet who with hope and faith in God, rise again"; three movements with "Recitatives," (duo dialogues) between them. Difficult.

I. "Andantino"; A Minor, 3/4 (quarter = 80); jaunty, rhythmic theme with a three-note motive permeating the movement; very brief, slow middle section in which violin and cello double the melody four octaves apart.

"Recitative no. 1 (Piano tacet)"; no key, changing meter, "Adagio" (quarter = 52); dialogue begun by violin playing a spiritual-like tune in harmonics (call and response, modal scale); cello replies with oscillating melodic fifths on D; the two instruments dialogue, using fragments of the "spiritual" theme, and another skipping, dotted-note theme which reappears in the third movement; they close on a second, D and E.

II. "Adagio"; 3/4 (quarter = 52); regular, slow rhythmic pulse; piano opens holding the same notes, D and E which ended the Recitative; cello begins a sequence of two-note phrases expanding upward from D, first a minor second, then a major second, minor third, to a major third; violin answers with falling two-note phrases while the piano takes the upward sequence; this theme is developed using different intervals, doublings, parallel and contrary motion, etc.; faint references to the theme of the first movement; cadences very firmly on an E Major triad.

"Recitative no. 2 (Piano tacet): changing meters, "Allegro"; violin opens dialogue again, with oscillating melodic thirds (reminiscent of first dialogue), leading to the skipping, dotted-rhythm melodic fragment; cello answers with the fragment; they "improvise" (written out) on both the skipping melody and the oscillating thirds; "spiritual" theme emerges again.

III. "Lento"; changing meters (quarter = 48-50); piano opens with oscillating melodic fifths on low C; fragments of the various themes are answered back and forth and combined in a synthesis; tempo gradually accelerates; cadences on tonic C.

(Composer, Anderson, Carter, Cohen, Roach)

Holt, Nora Douglas (Nora Lena James)

b. 1885 in Kansas City, Kansas; d. January 1974 in Los Angeles. Journalist, critic, organist, singer, and composer. Her musical education was obtained from Western University at Quindaro, Kansas, and the Chicago Musical College, where she studied with Felix

Borowsky and was the first black musician to earn the master's degree in 1918. She also studied with Nadia Boulanger at Fontainebleau, France, in 1931. She was a church organist in Kansas City, Missouri, before moving to Chicago around 1914. There she became one of the founders of the National Association of Negro Musicians in 1919, and music critic for the *Chicago Defender* from 1917-1921. She also published a magazine, *Music and Poetry*, from 1919-1921. For the next fifteen years she lived abroad, traveling widely and singing at parties and nightclubs. In 1938, she returned to the United States, living for three years in Los Angeles. She then settled in New York, where she was music critic for the *Amsterdam News* and had a classical music radio program on WLIB. Her compositions numbering some 200 works were all lost while she was abroad, and included a symphonic work, *Rhapsody on Negro Themes*, as well as four quartets and many songs.

Solo:
   Four Negro Dances, and other pieces.

Selected Bibliography:
Dannett, Sylvia. *Profiles in Negro Womanhood*. Vol. 2, 144–149. New York: Negro Heritage Library, 1966.
Spearman, Rawn. W. "Music Criticism of Nora Douglas Holt in *The Chicago Defender*, Saturday Edition, 1917-1923." *Black Music Research Bulletin* 12, no. 2 (Fall 1990):20.
(Correspondence with Rawn Spearman, Carter, Cohen, SouBD, etc.)

Johns, Altona Trent

b. 1904; d. 1977. Educator, pianist, and composer. Collaborated with Undine Smith Moore in founding the Black Music Center at Virginia State University in 1969–1972.

Solo:
   Barcarolle, published by Handy Brothers Music Publishers; unlocated.
   There's No Hiding Place Down Here

(Cohen, Roach)

King, Betty Jackson

b. 17 February 1928 in Chicago, Illinois. Choral conductor, educator, pianist, and composer. She began music training as a child with her mother Gertrude Jackson Taylor, and sang in the Jacksonian Trio with her mother and sister, Catherine. She attended Wilson Junior College, receiving inspiration and instruction there from Esther Goetz Gilliland, and completed her B.Mus (1950) and M.Mus (1952) at Chicago Musical College of Roosevelt University, studying voice with Thelma Waide Brown, composition with Hans Tischler and Karel Jirak and piano with Saul Dorfman. She also studied at Oakland University in Michigan, Glassboro College in New Jersey, the Peabody Conservatory in Baltimore, Maryland and the Westminster Choir College, Princeton, New Jersey. She taught at the University of Chicago Laboratory School, Roosevelt University in Chicago, Dillard University in New Orleans and the public schools in Wildwood, New Jersey, and has been active as a choir director in Chicago and at the Riverside Church in New York City. From 1979 to 1984 she was President of the National Association of Negro Musicians, Inc. She has been a guest clinician for the Carl Fischer Choral Workshop, Alabama Center for Higher Education, Jackson State University, South Carolina State University, University of Ohio, Delaware State University, and the University of San Diego. Her awards include the Governor's Teaching Award in New Jersey, Outstanding Secondary Educators of America, and a Proclamation for Women Composers from Mayor Harold Washington of Chicago. Her arrangements of spirituals were included on a Carnegie Hall special program of spirituals for Public Broadcasting and Television by Kathleen Battle and Jessye Norman in May 1990. In June 1991 she was honored by a three-day Music Fest dedicated to her and her music, including an "All Betty Jackson King Concert," at St. Mark United Methodist Church in Chicago. She began composing seriously in college and has written many choral works, art songs, and arrangements of spirituals. Her oratorio, *Saul of Tarsus,* was widely performed after its premiere in 1952 by Chicago's Imperial Opera Company, and the cantata, *Simon of Cyrene,* and choral work, *My Servant Job,* are also frequently performed. Her style is marked by an extended harmonic language, polytonal ambiguity of key, thick massive chord clusters, and simultaneous layers of sound. Her compositions are available through Jacksonian Press, Inc., P.O. Box 1556, Wildwood, N.J. 08260.

Solo:

> *Aftermath* (A Tone Poem), 1950, dedicated to Linnie Welch Freeman and prefaced with a poem by Elizabeth B. Widel, "I wish that I could grieve for what is done," about the

aftermath of destructive anger, the "numbness," "exhaustion," "grief" and "regret"; 10 pp.; B Minor, 4/4, "Adagio"; dramatic, rhetorical introduction to a lyrical theme accompanied by L.H. triplet arpeggios, then second theme building to a stormy climax before a calmer contrasting, questioning passage in ambiguous keys; returns to first two themes stated *fff* before a quiet, resigned ending; polytonal harmonies. Moderately difficult.

Four Seasonal Sketches, 1955, a suite ; 12 pp. 8 min.; each movement approx. 2 min. in length; can be played alone or together without much break between them. Each of the pieces is progressively more dramatic, thick and polytonal.

1. "Spring Intermezzo" A Major, 4/4; three part form; rhapsodic, gently sweeping; the R.H. melody rises out of L.H. arpeggiation, leading to undulating double thirds, and a middle section in F-sharp Major; a single flowing fabric rather than contrast; rich harmonies, but more clearly tonal than other pieces by King. Moderate. (Published in *Black Women Composers: A Century of Piano Music,* see Appendix 1.)

2. "Summer"; E Minor, 2/4, "Cantabile"; more polytonal and biting; some jazzy rhythms; middle section more contrasting, "Piu animato"; thickening chord textures and big climax (a summer storm); reference to opening theme at end. Moderately difficult.

3. "Autumn"; D Minor, 4/4; L.H. features a steady quarter note accompaniment throughout, starting single notes, then in fifths, octaves, suggesting Indian drums, (thus Indian summer); melody above it also starts in single notes, then in double thirds, octaves, and massive, polytonal chord clusters, returning to single notes at end. Moderate.

4. "Winter"; G Minor, 4/4; begins "Maestoso," with repeated pedal points on G in bass, chords with open fifths rising austerely above; rapid repeated notes and chords convey shimmery, icy cold, builds to a climax with large, sweeping rolled chords. Difficult.

Cradle Song, 1955
Reflections
Fantastic Mirror

Mother Goose Parade, c. 1971, dedicated to piano teacher, Saul Dorfman, at Chicago Musical College of Roosevelt University; 6 pp; polytonal, basically 4/4, "Martial"; four descending L.H. triads in root position provide the motives for much of the piece; consists of nursery tunes ("Mary had a Little Lamb," "Three Blind Mice," etc.) set against repetitive accompaniment patterns, and chordal transitional passages drawing on the opening motives. Moderate.

Ensemble:

> *A Cycle of Life* (Suite), violin and piano, 1953 -1988, for violinist Ron Clark; this work is not yet available, as of August 1991; about 15 min.; five movements corresponding to the cycle of individual as well as group (racial) life .
>
> 1. "Preface - Chant"; stark, primitive violin melody supported by piano in open hollow fifths.
> 2. "Threshold - Lullaby"; B flat Minor, 6/8; "Lento assai"; violin melody flows freely in varying rhythmic values and intervals over undulating bass with off-beat R.H. chords; contrasting middle section marked "Leggiero"; playful, builds gently before a brief closing reference to the opening theme and accompaniment. Moderately difficult.
> 3. "Statement - Blues."
> 4. "Fragment - Spiritual"; an unusual treatment of "This Little Light of Mine" in minor key, 5/4 quarter notes, to which is soon added a faster flowing counterpoint in a different key; the ambiguity of tonality and rhythm results in a striking evolution of this seemingly simple melody.
> 5. "Finale"; a canon for three voices; furious and dissonant.

Selected Bibliography:

Current, Gloster B. "National Association of Negro Musicians at 60-and Still Rolling Along!" *The Crisis*, (December 1979):411-415.

(Composer, Carter, Cohen, Holly, SouBD, SouMBA, Williams, etc. King is also listed in Evelyn White's *Choral Music by Afro-Americans*, and has been featured in articles in *Ebony*, October 1982, *Jet*, August 1982 and *Gospel Magazine*, January 1983.)

Kinney, L. Viola

b. around 1890 in Sedalia, Missouri. Teacher and composer. She attended Western University at Quindaro, Kansas, studying harmony and choral music with Robert Jackson. She taught music and English for 35 years (1911–1946) in Sedalia's segregated Lincoln High School, which changed its name to C. C. Hubbard High School (after its principal) in 1944. She married Fred Ferguson, an undertaker, in 1917 or 1918, and they were separated in 1925 (she resumed her maiden name in 1929). No other musical compositions by her have been located. *Mother's Sacrifice* was a prize winner at the Inter-State Literary Society Original Music Contest in 1908.

Solo:
> *Mother's Sacrifice,* c. 1909 by Albert Ross and Robert Jackson, with a photo of the composer on the cover; 4 pp.; F Major, 4/4 "Andante cantabile"; form is A B C D B^1 A^1 with a six-measure introduction; middle sections C and D are in 3/4, G Minor and E flat Major; last A section varies melody, its repeat is in bass clef with L.H. accompaniment crossing over; B sections are modulatory, bravura passage-work; changes of mood and pace, harmonic color (lowered VI, etc.). Moderate. (Located at Library of Congress, reserve storage #C202688. Published in *Black Women Composers: A Century of Piano Music,* see Appendix 1.)

(LCWh, State Historical Society of Missouri)

Larkins, Ida

b. late-nineteenth century. Performer and composer. She collaborated with her husband, John Larkins, in writing and publishing syncopated coon songs in New York. Two of these, dating from 1898, survive at the Library of Congress: "The Trolley Party in the Sky" and "Miss Hazel Brown." Her name alone appears on this solo piano piece which is sedate and ladylike, also located at the Library of Congress.

Solo:
> *Wild Flowers,* published 1905 in Chicago by the Pioneer Publishing Company; 4 pp.; G Major, 3/4 "Andante con expressione"; slow, sentimental waltz in rondo form Aa Ba Bb Ba C Ba D Ba; eight measure introduction and sixteen measure A section; B section closing with eight measures of A (Ba); repeated "dolce" without A, melody in L.H. (Bb); a new C section, sixteen measures; Ba is repeated *ff* "Grandioso"; D section, sixteen measures "Brilliante con delicatezzo"; concluding with D. S. al Fine (Ba). Moderate. (Located at the library of Congress, call number M25.L.)

(LCWh)

León, Tania Justina

b. 14 May 1943 in Havana, Cuba. Pianist, conductor, teacher and composer. She credits her grandmother with recognizing her early talent at age four, finding her a piano. and enrolling her in the conservatory. Her musical training was obtained at the Carlos Alfredo Peyrellade Conservatory, Havana (B.A., piano and theory, 1961), the National Conservatory, Havana (music education, 1964), and New York University (B.S., composition, 1971, M.S., 1973). In 1969 she co-founded the Dance Theater of Harlem with Arthur Mitchell and was its music director until 1980. She studied conducting with Laszlo Halasz, coaching with Leonard Bernstein and Seiji Ozawa at Tanglewood in 1978, and is presently associate conductor of the Brooklyn Philharmonic, whose Community Concert Series she founded in 1977. She is on the faculty of Brooklyn College, and has served as Resident Composer for the Lincoln Center Institute as well as Artistic Director of Composers' Forum in New York City. She has also worked extensively in musical theater, directing *The Wiz* on Broadway (1978) and Robert Wilson's *Death, Destruction and Detroit* (1979) as well as his *The Golden Windows* (1982) for which she composed the music. She has received numerous awards: the New York State Council on the Arts, Meet the Composer, the National Endowment of the Arts, and the American Academy and Institute of Arts and Letters, among others. Her works have been commissioned by the Dance Theater of Harlem, American Composers Orchestra, the Bay Area Women's Philharmonic, the Da Capo Chamber Players, National Public Radio, Solisti Chamber Orchestra of New York, Cincinnati Symphony Orchestra, and many other groups. Her compositions include orchestra pieces, ballets, theater works, instrumental solo and ensemble works. The *Spiritual Suite,* for narrator, two sopranos, chorus, and mixed ensemble, was premiered in 1976 with Marian Anderson as narrator. The ballet, *Dougla,* composed with Geoffrey Holder in 1974, was taken on tour in Europe and performed by the Harlem Dance Theater in the Soviet Union in 1988. Her works blend her Afro-Cuban, Hispanic and Latin-jazz heritage with international contemporary techniques in a highly sophisticated musical language. They are published by Peer-Southern Concert Music and distributed through the Theodore Presser Company, Presser Place, Bryn Mawr, PA 19010 (215) 527-4242. Some of her compositions (indicated below) can be borrowed from the American Music Center, 30 West 26th Street, Suite 1001, New York, N.Y. 10010-2011 (212) 366-5263.,

Solo:

> *Ensayos sobre una Toccata (Essays on a Toccata)*, 1966; ms.; 1 p.;
> an early stage in the development of León's compositional
> style, already showing the pointillistic octave displace-
> ments in alternating hands typical of her toccata passages.
> Moderate. (AMC call number M22 L579 P5.)

> *Homenaje a Prokofiev (Homage to Prokofiev)*, n.d., also early;
> ms.; 2 pp.; a morosely sardonic waltz reminiscent of
> Prokofiev's "wrong note" style. Moderate. (AMC call num-
> ber M32 L579 H7.)

> *Momentum*, 1984, published by Peer-Southern Publishing Co.;
> commissioned by the Women Composers Congress, Mexico;
> written for Yolanda Liepa and dedicated to Joan Tower; 8
> pp., 6 min.; atonal, free unmetered and variable meters;
> rhapsodic "Adagio" introduction starts slowly, accelerates
> to a motoric toccata section, returns to "Adagio ad lib.";
> some jazz harmonies and melodic "riffs"; opens and closes
> with a stopped low B-flat, her only use of inside-piano.
> Difficult. (AMC call number M25 L579 M7.)

> *Preludes nos. 1 and 2* , 1966; published in *Black Women
> Composers: A Century of Piano Music*. see Appendix 1.
> (AMC call number M22 L579 P5.):

>> "Sorpresa" (*"Surprise"*); 1 p; D Minor, 2/4; playful melodic
>> exchange between hands; surprise ending. Moderate.

>> "Pecera" (*"Aquarium"*); 1 p; atonal, 3/4, 2/4, "Sempre
>> Adagio"; languid, plaintive melody in L.H. and
>> unusual R.H. accompanying figuration were used a
>> decade later in the last movement of the *Concerto
>> Criollo*. Moderately difficult (difficult stretches).

> *Rituál*, 1987, published by Peer-Southern Publishing Co.;
> commissioned by Affiliate Artists Inc., dedicated to Arthur
> Mitchell and Karel Shook, performed by Joanne Polk at
> New York City's Alternative Museum Concert in February,
> 1989; title inspired by Buddhist chanting; 10 pp., 5 min. 45
> sec.; atonal, predominantly 6/8 (variable); begins "Lento
> serioso e rubato" gradually accelerating to "Avante e
> deciso" and continuing to accelerate to the end in driving
> percussive eighth notes; widely disjunct single notes inter-
> spersed with clangorous minor sevenths, ninths and seconds
> (her characteristic intervals). Difficult.

Ensemble:

> *A La Par*, piano and percussion, 1986, commissioned by the
> Whitney Museum; 15 min.; 3 movements, fast, slow fast; the

middle slow movement begins and ends freely and rhapsod-
ically, enclosing a Cuban dance, the guaguanco; its complicated rhythmic ostinato is juxtaposed against other
rhythmic patterns. Difficult.

Concerto Criollo, solo piano, solo timpani and orchestra, 1977
commissioned by the National Endowment for the Arts; 20
min. Difficult. (AMC call number M1040 L579.)

    I. "Allegro Moderato"; A-flat key signature, 12/8; highly
chromatic harmonies; brilliant, coloristic, virtuoso
piano part; Latin American rhythms; section marked
"meno mosso" begins with a piano solo "cantabile"
before it is rejoined by the orchestra.

    II. "Andante rubato"; A Major, 6/8; the piano is featured,
"sempre cantabile," in a folk-like melody with languid
grace-notes and syncopated rhythms.

    III. "Allegro"; F Minor, 4/4; rhythmic, driving, motoric toc-
cata; "Meno mosso" section with syncopated melodic
line by piano employs a brief passage from the early
Prelude no. 2 (1966).

Kabiosile, piano and orchestra, 1988, commissioned by the
American Composers Orchestra, premiered by Ursula
Oppens; 7 min.; composer's comment: "This piece is a salute
to my ancestors and the power they gave me to do what I
have chosen to do—which is music."; begins with a one
minute unmeasured piano cadenza; horns enter explosively,
then strings, etc.; León's comment on piano part: "like
flames of fire, with ever-changing shapes of constant
heat." Difficult.

Parajota Delaté, quintet: flute, clarinet, cello, violin, piano,
1988, commissioned by the Da Capo Chamber Players and
dedicated to Joan Tower; 3 min.; rhapsodic; instruments
interweave; pointillistic at times, each instrument has
moments of prominence; jazz influence. Difficult.

Pet's Suite, flute and piano, 1979, commissioned by Composers'
Forum; 23 pp., 20 min.; eight pieces named after pets; uses
unorthodox techniques (rhythms drummed inside-piano
with hard sticks and soft mallets, strumming, palm
clusters) as well as regular keyboard techniques and
humorous rubato to imitate pets' sounds and personalities:
"Kittens and Scrubbles," "Bonnie," "Ulfa and Muffin,"
"Ketty. . . Delilah. . . Henry," "Mei San," "Dulcie, Jeremy,"
"Prince," "Buttons and Smaller." Difficult.

Tones, piano and orchestra, 1977, commissioned by the Harlem Dance Theater, one of her first large works; unpublished; 4 min. 20 sec.; atonal, percussive, driving.

Selected Bibliography:
Iadavia-Cox, Angela. "The Tug Between Conducting and Composing." *Essence* (December 1976).
Lundy, Anne. "Conversations with Three Symphonic Conductors." *Black Perspective in Music 16, no. 2* (Fall 1988).
Mandel, Howard. "Tania León: Beyond Borders." *Ear Magazine* (December/January 1989).
(Composer, AMC, ASCAP, Carter, Cohen, Handy, Holly, SouBD, Peer-Southern promotion literature, etc.)

McLin, Lena Johnson

b. 5 September 1929 in Atlanta, Georgia. Choral conductor, educator, pianist, and composer. Her family was very musical and during her childhood, she lived for several years in the Chicago home of her uncle, Thomas A. Dorsey, the "Father of Gospel Music." At that time, she was cared for by her grandmother who told her about life under slavery and sang slave songs to her. These were important early influences on her musical style. In 1951 she completed her B.Mus. degree in piano at Spelman College, Atlanta, Georgia, despite surgery on a bone tumor in right hand. She credits her recovery to the care and skill of her piano teacher, Florence Brinkman Boynton. She won a scholarship to continue studies at the American Conservatory in Chicago where she studied theory and composition under Stella Roberts. She did extensive graduate work at Roosevelt University, studying voice with Thelma Waide Brown, as well as theory, composition, and electronic music. She taught music for many years in the Chicago public secondary schools, organized and directed the pilot music program at Kenwood Academy High School (1970–1991), composed rock music for high school groups, and conducted choral workshops in many states. She is the author of a music history text book, *Pulse: A History of Music* (Niel Kjos Publishing Company, 1977) and has produced a film, *The Origin of the Spiritual*. Her religious and secular choral works (which are published and widely performed) show the influence of her early gospel background. Her cantata, *Free at Last* (1964) in memory of Martin Luther King, Jr., has been performed in Carnegie Hall and was performed and recorded in Italy by Irene Oliver in 1989. She has also composed operas and instrumental works. Her piano pieces are unpublished and can be requested from her: 6901 Oglesby St., Chicago, IL 60649.

Solo:
> *Agreement March*, n.d.; 4 pp.; originally intended for wedding march.
>
> *Impressions*, 1957.
>
> *Song in C Minor*
>
> *A Summer Day*, composed in the 1970s; 3 pp. 3 min.; A Major, 6/8; three part form; improvisatory and languidly impressionistic in style; harmonies illustrate her original, characteristic varieties of seventh and ninth chords and her love of clusters of seconds. Moderate. (Published in *Black Women Composers: A Century of Piano Music*, see Appendix 1.)

Selected Bibliography:

DeGenova, Al. "Lena McLin: Music Power." *Upbeat Magazine* (May 1983):28–29.

Green, Mildred Denby. "Lena McLin." Chap. 6 of *Black Women Composers: A Genesis*. Boston: Twayne Publishing Co., 1983.

McLin, Lena Johnson. "Black Music in Church and School." In *Black Music in Our Culture*, edited by Dominique-René De Lerma, 35–41. Kent, OH, 1970.

Winer, Linda. "Kenwood High's Little Lady of Music." *Chicago Tribune*. (1970).

(Composer, Carter, Cohen, Holly, Meggett, SouBD, Roach, etc.)

McSwain, Augusta Geraldine

b. 4 May 1917 in Omaha, Nebraska. Pianist, teacher and composer. She graduated from Booker T. Washington High School in Enid, Oklahoma in 1933, and received her Bachelor of Arts and Bachelor of Music degrees from Bishop College in Marshall, Texas in 1937 and 1938. She attended Northwestern University in Evanston, Illinois, where she earned the Master of Music degree in 1943. She studied piano with Helen Hagan (see entry for Hagan) in the 1930s, as well as with Raymond Morris in Hartford, Connecticut, and Kurt Wanjeck in Chicago, Illinois, and made numerous appearances as a concert pianist. She joined the faculty at Bishop College in 1938 and became Dean of its Music School in 1945. She composed choral works, songs, a string quartet and several piano pieces. She has retired and teaches piano privately. Her works may be requested from her at 419 East State St., Enid, OK 73701.

Solo:
> *The Chase*, n.d.; 2 pp.; C Major, mixed meters, no indication; L.H. melody, accompanied by agitated, off-beat, eighth note, major second intervals in R.H.; dance-like, with scurrying runs up and down the keys, alternating hands on sixteenths. Easy to moderate.
>
> *Passacaglia in E Minor*, 1960; 3 pp.; 3/4, "Lento"; ternary form; R.H. melody accompanied by steady, flowing eighth L.H.; middle section has new L.H. melody; short coda with both hands in eighths. Moderate.
>
> *Rustic Dance*, n.d., "To Willie Jean Smith"; 2 pp.; F Major, 2/4, "Giocoso - Moderato"; A B A C A form; A section in march-like chords, "Marcato," featuring parallel fifths; alternating section B marked "Nostalgia," and section C marked "Cantabile e expressivo." Moderate.

(Composer, Carter, Cohen)

Manggrum, Loretta Cessor

b. 1896 in Gallipolis, Ohio.   Pianist, organist, teacher and composer.   She earned the B.Mus. degree from Ohio State University in 1951 at age 55, and the M.Mus. degree, as the first black student at that institution, from the Cincinnati Conservatory of music in 1953.   She also attended Fisk University, Capitol University in Chicago, and the Royal Conservatory of Music in Toronto, Canada, studying composition there with Roy Harris. She concertized as an organist and taught in the the Cincinnati Public Schools.   In 1980 at age 84 she began full-time studies toward the D.M.A. and was awarded an honorary doctorate by the University of Cincinnati in 1984.   She was named "Woman of the Year" by the Cincinnati Enquirer in 1978.   Her collected works are housed at the Library of Congress (Acquisitions #B09/913E/SA/Sh2) and include six cantatas, numerous choral works and arrangements of spirituals, and a number of piano solos.   They can be seen, but are under copyright and do not have permission for photocopy.

Solo:
> *Expression*, c. 1984; 6 pp.; A-flat Major, 3/4, "Moderately Fast/ Lively"; more chromatic and adventurous than her other pieces; key change to D major. Moderate.
>
> *Happy and Gay*, c. 1980; 3 pp.; D Minor, 3/4, (quarter = 126); R.H. melody and L.H. skips; some eighths hands together.

Moderately easy.

Melody in A (listed, but not located)

Melody in Octaves, c. 1980; 3 pp.; G Major, 4/4, no indication; both hands in broken octaves in eighths, a third apart, both parallel and contrary motion.

Mountain Climbing (listed but not located)

Piano Variations, n.d.; 5 pp.; D Major, 3/4 "Adagio Cantabile"; a sixteen measure theme and four variations; L.H. melody and R.H. arpeggiation which is varied; one of the variations has the melody in the R.H. Moderate.

Rippling Waves, c. 1980; 5 pp.; E-flat major, 3/4, "Andantino"; introduction, then R.H. melody in octaves, and chords, with eighth figuration. Moderate.

Roaming, c. 1980; 3 pp.; F Major, 3/4, "Adagio" (quarter = 126); ternary form; middle section in B-flat, slower. Easy to Moderate.

Skipping, c. 1981; 2 pp.; A Minor, 2/4, "Lively/ Adagio" (sic) (quarter = 100); R.H. melody in dotted rhythms, ornamented; L.H. quarters in wide skips. Moderate.

Selected Bibliography:

Rieselman, Deborah. "A Mind for Music." *Horizons* (May 1989):8–13.

"Focus: '88 - The Black Arts." Program of events by The Cincinnati Chapter of the Links, Inc., 1988.

(LC)

Martin, Delores J. Edwards

b. 18 July 1943 in Los Angeles, California. Pianist and composer. She began piano studies at age four and was a student of Erica Zador at the University of Southern California Preparatory Department. Her B.A. in music theory was completed at Pepperdine University where she studied composition with Joseph Wagner. She also earned a Diploma in composition from the American Academy, Paris, France. She is a member of the American Society of Composers, Authors and Publishers, International League of Women Composers, and Mu Phi Epsilon. Her works include commercial and popular music and her popular song, "Winds of Change," took Honorable Mention in the Composers Guild contest in Salt Lake City, Utah in 1983. Her compositions may be obtained from her at 3760 Bays Ferry Way, Marietta, Georgia 30062.

Solo:

Circle of Dreams, c. 1974; 4 and 1/2 pp., 4 min.; C Major, 4/4, "Moderato" (eighth = 126); free fantasy style in ternary form; parallel fourths and fifths "written in dedication to all theory teachers who tell you they should be avoided." Moderately difficult.

Un Jour, c. 1971, published by Soundwork, in Seattle, Washington in 1979; 11 pp., 7 min.; three movements depicting times of day. Moderately difficult.

1. "Matin" ("Morning"); F Major, 3/4, "Moderato" (eighth = 152); busy air of morning activities; suggests a fanfare.
2. "Après Midi" ("Afternoon"); F Minor, 6/4, "Andante" (quarter = 96); contrapuntal treatment of several different ideas, including a fragment of a Christmas carol and a Bach-style fugal passage.
3. "Nuit" ("Night"); D-flat Major, 6/8, "Andante" (eighth = 126); nocturne with contrasting lively middle section.

Tribute to Edward Hopper, The Artist, in progress.

Ensemble:

La Mer Turbulente (The Restless Sea), two pianos, c. 1973; 6 pp., 2 min.; C Minor, 4/4, "Agitato" (quarter = 72); "an exercise for two pianos playing as one"; very tonal; straightforward; chords, turns, and runs; ternary form. Moderate.

(Composer, Cohen, also listed in Stern's *Performing Arts Directory,* 1991, 1992, New York: published by Robert Stern.)

Moore, Dorothy Rudd

b. 4 June 1940 in New Castle, Delaware. Composer, singer and poet. She began music studies with Harry Andrews at Howard High School in Wilmington, Delaware and took piano lessons at the Wilmington School of Music. Her B.A. in theory and composition was completed *magna cum laude* in 1963 at Howard University, where she studied composition with Mark Fax. She was the recipient of a Lucy Moten Fellowship for study with Nadia Boulanger at the American Conservatory in Fontainebleau, France, in 1963, and continued composition studies with Chou Wen-Chung in New York in 1965. She taught at the Harlem School of the Arts, New York University, and the Bronx Community College, and was one of the founders of the Society of Black Composers in 1968. She is active as a singer with the Lola Hayes Studio in New York City, and writes poetry. Five of her poems have been set to music by her husband,

cellist/ composer Kermit Moore. She usually composes in response
to commissions for specific ensembles, and has received grants from
Meet the Composer, the American Music Center, and the New York
State Council on the Arts. Many of her works, such as the *Baroque
Suite* (1965) for solo cello, and *Dirge and Deliverance* (1971) for
cello and piano, were written for Kermit Moore. Among her best-
known compositions are *From the Dark Tower* (1970), eight songs on
texts by black American poets for mezzo-soprano, cello and piano,
and *Weary Blues* (1972, published in Patterson) for baritone, cello
and piano on a text of Langston Hughes. Both works have been
arranged for voice and orchestra. Other works are *Sonnets on Love,
Rosebuds, and Death* (1976) for soprano, violin, and piano, *Flowers
of Darkness* (1990) for tenor and piano, and *Moods* (1969) for viola
and cello. Her opera on her own libretto, *Frederick Douglass*, was
completed in 1985 and performed by Opera Ebony at Aaron Davis
Hall of the City College of New York. Moore's works are
characterized by dramatic intensity and seriousness of tone,
dissonant counterpoint and quartal harmonies. Her compositions
can be purchased from American Composers Alliance, 170 W. 74th
St., New York, N.Y. 10023 (212) 362-8900, and some (indicated
below) can be borrowed from the American Music Center, 30 West
26th Street, Suite 1001, New York, N.Y. 10010-2011 (212) 366-5263.

Solo:

> *Dream and Variations,* 1974, written for Ludwig Olshansky and
> first performed by Zita Carno at Carnegie Recital Hall,
> February 1975; 21 pp., 18 min.; slow, dramatic introduction
> over a low D pedal point; dreamy waltz followed by a
> fantasy of loosely constructed variations; sudden shifts and
> juxtapositions of textures and moods. Difficult. (AMC call
> number M52 M821 D7.)
>
> *A Little Whimsy,* 1978, a teaching piece; 4 pp., 2 min.; C Major,
> 4/4 "Allegro" (half note = 80); witty and humorous; wry,
> skipping L.H. ostinato and contrasting, romantic waltz
> keep interrupting each other; cadences to unexpected keys.
> Moderate. (Published in *Black Women Composers: A
> Century of Piano Music,* see Appendix 1.)

Ensemble:

> *Dirge and Deliverance,* cello and piano; 1971, first performed
> by Kermit Moore, cello, and Zita Carno, piano, at Alice
> Tully Hall, May 1972; 23 pp., 16 min. Difficult. (AMC call
> number M233 M821 D5.)
>
> 1. "Dirge "; 2/2, "Adagio" (half note = 44); piano begins

with sombre chords; cello theme with three-note motive representing human spirit longing to be free.

2. "Deliverance"; 4/8, "Allegro" (eighth = 126); cello begins alone; three-note motive transformed, angry; extended cello cadenza (written out); resolved ending.

Night Fantasy, clarinet and piano, 1978; 21 pp., 10 min.; in two movements. Difficult.

I. "Largo"; (quarter = 52); one-minute solo piano introduction; opening chord's intervals (half-step and fourth) permeate the melodic and harmonic fabric of the movement; intense, dramatic gestures; dialogue and exchange with clarinet; short, forceful phrases in irregular rhythms; return of opening motives.

II. "Allegro"; (eighth = 160); lively, staccato, more continuous sixteenth-note motion; recurring motive of falling half-step and minor third; "meno mosso" section with regular 3/8 pulse; another contrasting "Andante" section (quarter = 96); gradual return of opening motives and motion; terse, rhetorical.

Three Pieces for Violin and Piano; 1967, commissioned by Richard Elias and performed by Elias, violinist and David Garvey, pianist, at Carnegie Recital Hall, New York City, March 1967; 8 pp., 10 min. Difficult. (AMC call number M221 M821 P7.)

1. "Vignette"; 6/8, "Moderato" (dotted quarter = 60); 3 pp.; casual, insouciant violin melody with wide-ranging skips, over gently rhythmic chordal accompaniment; more aggressive middle passage with quartal, tritone melodic intervals and harmonies; exchange of material between instruments.

2. "Episode"; 4/4, "Molto Adagio" (quarter = 40); 2 pp.; spare, mysterious, intensely expressive; piano opens with long-held major third on E-flat, gradually adds notes downwards (D-flat, B, D); violin melody has wide skips, double stops; piece closes with piano's long-held major third on D against violin's high C (recalling intervallic motive of beginning).

3. "Caprice"; 6/4, "Presto" (dotted half = 100); playful, staccato; quartal, tritone chords and melodies; slower, "dolce" middle section in 3/4 with large skips .

Trio no. 1, piano, violin, cello; 1970, commissioned by the Reston Trio and first performed by them at Carnegie Recital Hall, New York City, March 1970; 36 pp., 15 min; in three movements. Difficult. (AMC call no. M312 M821 T8 no. 1.)

I. "Adagio"; 3/4 (quarter = 69); lyrical, linear counterpoint; opens with three-note motive in piano; winding, chromatic melodic lines; often doubled at octaves or sixth, giving open sound; often in triplets; contrasting, playful middle section (eighth = 138) uses motive from opening; becomes "pesante," leads back to opening three-note motive and recapitulation.

II. "Adagio"; 4/4 (quarter = 60); marked "Stark and Intense"; opens with piano theme doubled in octaves, later in parallel fifths and fourths; quartal chords; sinuous chromatic melody in triplets reminiscent of first movement; "attaca" the next movement:

III. "Presto agitato"; 4/8 (eighth = 118); parallel fourths reminiscent of second movement; much doubling at the octave; motoric sixteenth-note passage; contrapuntal fugal section; return of the parallel fourths and motoric sixteenth note passage building to the close.

Selected Bibliography:

Page, Tim. "Opera: World Premiere of 'Frederick Douglass.'" *The New York Times* (30 June 1985).

Tischler, Alice. "Dorothy Moore." In *Fifteen Black American Composers: A Bibliography of Their Works*, 201–212. Detroit: Information Coordinators, 1981.

(Composer, AMC, Block, Carter, Cohen, Holly, NGrDAM, Roach, Patterson, SouBD, SouMBA, Williams, etc.)

Moore, Undine Smith

b. 25 August 1904 in Jarrat, Virginia; d. 6 February 1989 in Petersburg, Virginia. Choral conductor, educator and composer. She was educated in the public schools in Petersburg, Virginia and began piano lessons at age seven with Lillian Allen Darden, a graduate of Fisk University, Nashville, Tennessee, who encouraged her to attend Fisk. She received the first scholarship given by the Juilliard School of Music to study music at Fisk and completed her B.A. *cum laude* , as well as a Diploma in music, in 1926. While there, she was a piano and organ student of Alice M. Grass. In 1931, she completed the M.A. degree and professional diploma at Teachers College, Columbia University in New York City, studying theory and composition with Howard Murphy. She also attended the Manhattan School of Music in New York City as well as the Eastman School of Music, Rochester, New York. She taught in the public schools of Goldsboro, North Carolina, where she was

Supervisor of Music and at Virginia State College (1927-1971), where she began to compose to meet the needs of the laboratory school chorus.   She was visiting professor at Virginia Union University in Richmond, Virginia as well as several Minnesota colleges: Carlton College in Northfield, St. Benedict College in St. Joseph, and St. Johns University in Collegeville.   She gave workshops and toured widely in West Africa and in the United States, and was co-founder, with Altona Trent Johns, of the Black Music Center at Virginia State College in 1969–1972.   She held honorary doctorates from Virginia State University (1972) and Indiana University (1976), and received many awards, including a Certificate of Appreciation from Mayor John Lindsay of New York City (1972), the Seventh Annual Humanitarian Award from Fisk University (1973), National Association of Negro Musicians Distinguished Achievement Award (1975), and the proclamation of an Undine Smith Moore Day on April 13, 1975 by Remmis Arnold, Mayor of Petersburg, Virginia.   She received the Governor's Award in the Arts and was also a Cultural Laureate for the state of Virginia.   Her influence was strong, and her former students include many celebrated musicians.   On 23–24 June 1990, a memorial "Undine Smith Moore Music Festival" was held in Winston-Salem, North Carolina.   She composed in a variety of forms and her compositional techniques range from conventional and tonal to atonal and twelve-tone (as in *Three Pieces for Flute and Piano*, 1958).   Her choral works are best-known, most notably, *Lord, We Give Thanks to Thee* (1971), *Daniel, Daniel, Servant of the Lord* (1952), and *The Lamb* (1958).   Her cantata for chorus, orchestra and soloists, *Scenes from the Life of a Martyr* (in memory of Martin Luther King, Jr.), was nominated for a Pulitzer Prize in 1981, and has been widely performed.   Her art song,"Love, Let the Wind Cry"(1961, published in Patterson) is frequently programmed.   Her late works include *Soweto* for violin, cello and piano (1987) in memory of the 1976 massacre in South Africa.   Information can be requested from her daughter, Mary Easter, 800 St. Olaf Ave., Northfield, MN 55057.

Solo:

> *Before I'd Be A Slave*, 1953, one of a group of pieces commissioned by Barbara Hollis for the Modern Dance Group, Virginia State College; 5 pp., 3 min.; dramatic and rhapsodic; opens with furious, intense drumming in the bass register; coloristic glissandi and tremolos; emergence of poignant theme, first four ascending notes, then repeated adding more, expanding upwards; composer's program: "The frustration and chaos of slaves who wish to be free - in the

depths - being bound - attempts to flee - tug of war with oppressors - continued aspiration - determination - affirmation." Difficult. (Published in *Black Women Composers: A Century of Piano Music*. See Appendix 1.)

Fugue in C Minor, n.d.; 3 pp.; F Major, 4/4; traditional, eighteenth-century counterpoint in three voices. Moderate.

Many Thousand Gone, c. 1986, composition for piano based on the slave song; 7 pp.; B-flat Major, 4/4; tonal, no dissonance; fantasy-style, featuring large chords, octaves, arpeggiated passage-work; massive sound. Moderately difficult.

Romantic Young Clown, 1952, "For Mary Hardie"; 4 pp., 3 min.; A Major, 4/4, "Scherzando" (quarter = 96); comment by composer: "This young clown is joyous and carefree!—Not at all the 'tears below the makeup,' Pagliacci type. Tho' he tries hard to sing a dignified love song, he cannot refrain from turning somersaults and 'cutting up,' unlike proper lovers who are often serious and sad." The mood alternates between wistfully expressive and gaily exuberant. Moderate.

Scherzo, 1930, previously titled *Prelude*; 3 pp.; F Major, 3/4, 4/4, 5/4 , "Very Fast" (quarter = 120-126); playful and mischievous, with slippery, shifting key and meter; less tonal and more dissonant than Moore's other short piano pieces. Moderate.

Ensemble:

Afro-American Suite, flute, cello, piano, 1969, commissioned by and dedicated to D. Antoinette Handy and the Trio Pro Viva, recorded by them on Eastern Record Company (see Discography); in four movements; richly orchestrated sound from all three instruments; at times dissonant and bitonal. Difficult.

   I. "Nobody Knows the Trouble I See, Lord"; 6 pp.; D Minor, 4/4, "Andante (very sustained)"; opens with cello melody over pianissimo piano quarter-note chords; duet as well as call and response between cello and flute; ponderous piano chords and two-note phrases in eighths.

   II. "I Heard the Preaching of the Elder, Preaching the Word of God"; 10 pp.; D Major, 2/4, "Allegro molto e marcato"; rhythmic, jubilant; exchanging and crisscrossing of thematic material

   III. "Who Is That Yonder? Oh, It Looks Like My Lord, Coming in a Cloud"; for alto flute; 7 pp.; D Minor, 4/4, "Adagio, ma appassionato"; opens with pianissimo piano chords in dotted, short-long rhythm; then expressive, improvisatory flute solo, becoming an exchange in dialogue with cello, and finally a duet in unison.

IV. "Shout All Over God's Heaven"; 8 pp.; D major, 4/4, "Allegro molto e marcato"; opens with flute solo, then rapid exchange and punctuation of melody among the three instruments.

Romance, two pianos, 1952; a "romantic, Godowsky-sounding piece, filled with too many diminished seventh chords," comment by the composer (Harris).

Soweto, for violin, cello and piano, 1987 commissioned and first performed by the Nova Trio, Norfolk, Virginia; in memory of the South African massacre at Soweto township in 1976; composer's comments: "I felt I did not choose the word [Soweto]. The word chose me." Difficult. (See Discography)

I. "Allegro giacoso"

II. "Allegro assai con brio"; 22 pp.; atonal, 4/4 (quarter = 72); composer's comment: "The piano is bold, aggressive, angry, fast, accented. The word 'Soweto' is the rhythmic motive, accent on the second syllable." Brilliant, demanding string parts; call and response passage between cello and violin, marked "espressivo"; middle section has composer's note to "create the effect of a collage" with cello melody superimposed on piano's dim, blurred background; ends with broad, majestic melody played in unison by violin and cello over piano's chordal "Soweto" motive.

Three Pieces for Flute (or clarinet) and Piano, 1958; premiere performance in Town Hall, New York City, September 1972: "Introduction" ("Pomposo"), "March," and "Dance" ("Allegro"); first and third movements use twelve-tone technique. (See Discography.)

Selected Bibliography:

Allen, Simona. Program notes for "A Concert of Music by Undine Smith Moore" presented by Winston-Salem Delta Fine Arts, Inc., 24 June 1990.

Baker, David N., Lida M. Belt, and Herman C. Hudson. 1978. "Undine Smith Moore." In *The Black Composer Speaks.*, 173–. Metuchen, N.J.: Scarecrow Press, 1978.

Harris, Jr., Carl. "Conversation with Undine Smith Moore, Composer and Master Teacher." *The Black Perspective in Music* 16, no. 1 (Spring 1985):79–86.

Moore, Undine Smith. n.d. An autobiographical lecture. Cambria Historical Archives Cassette C142. Cambria Records and Publishing, Box 374, Lomita, CA 90717.
(Carter, Cohen, Holly, NGrDAM, Patterson, Roach, SouBD, etc.)

Norman, Jeanette Latimer

n.d., n.p..

Solo:
> *A Day in the Life of a Child,* published by Carl Fischer in 1924; seven episodes. Easy.

(Carter)

Norman, Ruth

b. 12 February 1927 in Chicago, Illinois. Concert pianist, lecturer and composer. She grew up in Omaha, Nebraska, and received her musical education at Nebraska University (B.M.E.) and the Eastman School of Music (M.Mus.). She continued studies in piano with Evelyn Swarthout Hayes and Robert Dumm, and in composition with Russell Woollen, Esther Ballou and Robert Paris. Her professional background includes performing as organist as well as pianist, choral directing, musicology, and instrumental instruction on secondary and college levels. She has appeared as concert pianist at the Kennedy Center, the Corcoran Museum and the U.S. State Department among other places and has presented lecture-recitals on Black Composers at many schools including Yale University, Tufts University, and Virginia State College. She has received the Philip Stern Foundation Award as well as two grants from the National Endowment for the Arts. She has recorded two Opus One albums, on which her own compositions also appear. Her works include a symphony, choral and chamber works, notably *Prayer of St. Francis* for SATB chorus, and *Golden Precepts* for chamber ensemble and soprano. Her works are available from her at 7908 Orchid St. N.W., Washington, D.C. 20012.

Solo:
> **Autumn. 1979, "to Mildred Ellis"; 4 pp., 3 min.; A Minor, 4/4, no indication; two voices in legato, flowing eighth motion; middle section R.H. in double thirds; tonal, mildly dissonant. Moderate.**

Cosmic Journey, 1984; 10 pp., 6 and 1/2 min.; atonal, no time
    signature (numbers at beginning of each measure for quarter
    beats in measure), "Legato"; dramatic opening with
    chordal dotted-note rhythm; static and and mysterious
    quarter note motion in intervals and harmonies of seventh
    and minor ninths; middle section with more rapid sixteenth
    note movement; return to static chords building to a chordal
    climax before returning to quiet atmosphere of the opening.
    Difficult.

Fifteen Children's Pieces.:
    "Winter Days," 1979; 1 p.; A Minor, 4/4, (quarter = 80);
        ternary form with middle melody in L.H. Easy to
        moderate.
    "Tippy (my Teddy Bear)," 1976; 1 and 1/2 pp.; D Minor, 6/8,
        "Allegretto." Easy to moderate.
    "The Swing," 1976, "To Judy"; 2 pp.; G Major, 6/8, "Legato";
        legato eighth motion. Easy to moderate.
    "The Tea Party," n.d.; 1 and 1/2 pp.; C Major, mostly 3/4;
        begins by knocking inside piano and speaking while
        playing, announcing party; hands together, R.H.
        melody with L.H. accompaniment in two note slurs.
        Easy.
    "It's Raining," n.d.; 3 pp.; B Minor, 3/4, "Allegro"; staccato
        eighths and rests in treble range, at first together, then
        alternating; second section "Vivace"; Moderate.

Force Centres, n.d.; 8 pp., 6 and 1/2 min.; atonal, no key or time
    signature (numbers for quarter beats in measure); opens with
    rising glissando on strings inside-piano, held by pedal
    while counting to 51; indications referring to spiritual
    attunement, metaphysics, and chakras; trills and tremolos
    against melody played in parallel minor sevenths; har-
    monies based on fourths and tritones; two-part dissonant
    counterpoint; several changes of tempo leading to climactic
    break; returns to melodic motives of beginning. Difficult.

Four Preludes :
    "Prelude no. 1," 1969, "To Ruth Watanabe," recorded by
        Miss Norman on Opus One records, #35; 1 p.; no key
        signature, changing meter, (quarter = 60); marked
        "legato" and "cantabile"; flowing, continuous eighths;
        two voices, dissonant counterpoint. Moderately
        difficult.
    "Prelude no. 3, A Sketch," 1970; 2 pp.; no key signature, 5/8
        changing, "Andante" (eighth = 72); two voices; theme
        presented in canon; motives developed; return of theme

in unison, before parts separate in contrary motion; atonal, dissonant counterpoint. Moderately difficult.

"Prelude no. 4," 1980; 2 pp.; no key signature, changing meter, (quarter = 66), marked "sempre legato"; also in two voices; highly chromatic dissonant counterpoint; cumulative repetition of shorter motives; dynamic over-all shape. Moderately difficult.

Molto Allegro (Toccata), 1969, "To Pat and Ev Hayes"; Recorded by Miss Norman on Opus One, #35; 6 pp.; 3 min.; atonal, 4/4, "Allegro con spirito" (quarter = 76); rapid repeated sixteenth notes in L.H.; terse, fragmented R.H. melody in low register; climactic section in rugged quartal harmonies and ninths; highly charged. Difficult.

Festival Overture, for piano or organ

Introspection

Ensemble:

Capriccio, piano, violin and cello, n.d.; 10 pp., 5 and 1/2 min.; atonal, no key or time signature, (quarter = 56); opens with cello recitative in wide-ranging melodic contours, followed by a dialogue between cello and violin; piano provides a static envelope of widely-spaced harmonies based on tritones, ninths, etc.; a violin solo leads to a new section with more interaction among the three instruments; returns to the themes and texture of the opening. Difficult.

(Composer, Cohen, Roach)

Perry, Julia Amanda

b. 25 March 1924 in Lexington, Kentucky; d. 29 April 1979 in Akron, Ohio. Perry's father, a physician, was a pianist, and her two older sisters studied violin. The family moved to Akron when she was ten, and she took violin and piano lessons. She also studied voice with Mable Todd, who was a strong influence. After graduation from Akron High School, she attended Westminster Choir College in Princeton, New Jersey, where she studied piano, voice, violin, conducting and composition, completing her B.Mus. in 1947 (voice) and her M.Mus. (composition) in 1948. Her master's thesis was a secular cantata, *Chicago*, based on poems of Carl Sandburg. She moved to New York in 1948 and continued composition studies at the Juilliard School of Music. A sacred cantata, *Ruth*, was performed at the Riverside Church in April 1950. In 1951, she studied with Luigi Dallapiccola at the Berkshire Music Center in Lenox,

Massachusetts, and the next year she received a Guggenheim Fellowship for further work with him in Florence, Italy. She also studied with Nadia Boulanger in Paris, and won the Boulanger Grand Prix for her Viola Sonata. In 1954 she served as assistant coach at Columbia Opera Workshop in New York. Her one-act opera, *The Cask of Amontillado* (based on the short story by Edgar Allen Poe) was produced at the McMillan Theater at Columbia University that year. She received a second Guggenheim Fellowship in 1954, and returned to Italy to continue studies with Dallapiccola. In the summers of 1956, 1957, and 1958 she studied orchestral conducting at the Accademia Chigiana in Siena, Italy, and in 1957 she organized and presented a series of concerts in Europe under the auspices of the United States Information Service. She returned to the United States in 1959. She won the American Academy and National Institute of Arts and Letters Award in 1964, taught at Florida A & M College in 1967-68 and was a visiting lecturer at the Atlanta College Center in 1968-69. In 1971 she suffered a paralytic stroke and was ill for a number of years. She taught herself to write with her left hand and was able to return to composing (symphonies nos. 5–12, etc.) before she died in 1979. Besides the twelve symphonies, Perry's compositions include a violin concerto, two piano concertos, other instrumental and chamber works, and several operas, including *The Bottle*, *The Selfish Giant* (on Oscar Wilde's fable), and *The Symplegades* (about the seventeenth-century Salem witchcraft trials). Black musical idioms are evident in her early arrangements of spirituals and vocal works, and her later works are in an intensely lyrical neo-classic style, employing dissonance, quartal harmonies, cluster chords, and other twentieth-century compositional elements. Her large-scale structures display strong organizational qualities. The *Stabat Mater* (1951) for contralto and string orchestra or quartet, *Homunculus C.F.* (1960, see below) and *A Short Piece for Orchestra* for orchestra have been recorded (see Discography). A number of her songs were published by Galaxy Publishing Company and several of her chamber and orchestral works are available in facsimile editions from Peer-Southern Concert Music through Theodore Presser, Bryn Mawr, PA. 19010 (215) 527-4242. Of her solo piano music, only the two-page *Prelude* has been located. It is located, together with other works by Perry, at the American Music Center, 30 West 26th St., Suite 1001, New York, N.Y. 10010-2011 (212) 366-5263.

Solo:
   Lament, 1947; unlocated.

Pearls on Silk , 1947; unlocated.

Prelude for Piano, 1946, revised 1962; 2 pp.; C Minor, 3/4 "Slow" (quarter = 44); chordal, dissonant, sombre. Moderate. (Published in *Black Women Composers: A Century of Piano Music.* See Appendix 1.)

Suite of Shoes , 1947, unlocated.

Three Pieces for Children, unlocated.

Ensemble:

Concerto no. 2 for Piano and Orchestra, 1964; one movement; "Fast" (quarter = 116); brilliant, dynamically varied, technically difficult piece with much motoric passage-work and repeated patterns. Difficult (Available from Peer-Southern Concert Music, see above)

Concerto for Piano and Orchestra in Two Uninterrupted Speeds, 1969; the first "speed" is "Moderate" (eighth = 80); sparse texture of sustained single notes and chords with soft, muted dynamics and timbres; the second "speed" is a version of the *Concerto no. 2,* "Fast" (quarter = 116), and features the same motoric passage-work and brilliant dynamics. (Also available from Peer-Southern, see above.)

Homunculus C.F., harp, celesta, piano, and percussion, composed during the summer of 1960; the title refers to the medieval alchemy experiments in Goethe's *Faust* by the apprentice, Wagner, who brought to life a test tube-man, or *homunculus:* "an archetype seeking realization . . . a way to break from his test-tube phase and come into being"; C.F. refers to the chord of the fifteenth on which the composition is based: E G-sharp B D-sharp F-sharp A-sharp C-sharp,E-sharp; this chord appears only gradually, a few notes at a time, because, according to *Faust,* "one must approach the ideal by degrees, repeating nature's own process"; four sections. Difficult. (Recorded on CRI S-252, see Discography. Score available from Peer-Southern Concert Music through Theodore Presser Company, see above. Also published in James Briscoe, *Historical Anthology of Music by Women,* see Selected Bibliography, below.)

Section 1; unpitched percussion instruments; rhythmic canon employing retrograde rhythms.

Transition (measures 41–60); timpani introduce D-sharp, F-sharp, G-sharp.

Section 2; duet between timpani and harp; principally melodic elements E F-sharp G-sharp D-sharp; then a

> new motive with B E G-sharp and F-sharp.
>
> Section 3; harmonic, using E F-sharp B G-sharp and D-sharp.
>
> Section 4; combines harmony, melody and rhythm; entire C.F. (chord of the fifteenth) presented.
>
> *Viola Sonata,* viola or violin (?) and piano, 1952; won Boulanger Grand Prix; still unlocated.

Selected Bibliography:

Ammer, Christine. *Unsung: A History of Women in American Music,* 156–158. Westport, CT: Greenwood Press, 1980.

Green, Mildred Denby. "Julia Perry." Chap. 4 in *Black Women Composers: A Genesis.* Boston: Twayne Music Publishers, 1983.

————, "Julia Perry." In *Historical Anthology of Music by Women,* ed. by James Briscoe, 333–334. Bloomington, IL: Indiana University Press, 1987.

(AMC, Block, Carter, Cohen, Holly, Meggett, NegYB, NGrDAM, SouBD, Southall, Williams, etc.)

Perry, Zenobia Powell

b. 3 October 1914 in Boley, Oklahoma. Pianist, teacher and composer. At age fourteen, she was a special student in piano at the Eastman School of Music. She received her B.S. degree from Tuskegee Institute, Alabama in 1938, and her M.A. from the University of Northern Colorado in 1945. She holds an additional M.A. degree from the University of Wyoming where she studied piano and composition with Alan Willman and composition with Darius Milhaud. She also has been a student of Robert Nathaniel Dett, Gunnar Johansen, Charles Jones and Cortez Reese. She taught at Arkansas Agricultural, Mechanical, and Normal College from 1946 to 1955 and at Central State University at Wilberforce, Ohio from 1955 to her retirement in 1982. In April, 1986, she was Guest Composer at the Dana New Music Festival at Youngstown State University, Ohio, where some of her compositions were conducted by Dr. Jo Ann Lanier, whose doctoral dissertation at the American Conservatory of Music in Chicago, Illinois, was "The Concert Songs of Zenobia Powell Perry." She was honored in 1987 by the Ohioana Library Association with a Special Citation for her distinguished service to Ohio in the field of music. Her opera, *Tawawa House ,* was premiered at Central State University the same year. Several of her works were included on the programs of a "Symposium in Celebration of Black American Women in Music" at California State University in Northridge in 1987 and her *Four Mynyms for*

Three Players was also performed at the Smithsonian Institute in Washington, D.C. in 1988. In 1989, her piece for winds, percussion and narrator, *Ships That Pass in the Night*, was premiered at West Virginia University. Besides the opera, songs, and chamber works, Powell has composed a mass, and works for band and orchestra. Her style is primarily contrapuntal, tonal and mildly dissonant. Added sixths and clusters of seconds lend a jazz flavor to the harmonies, and her melodies are often folk-like. Her works may be obtained from the composer at P.O. Box 73, Wilberforce, OH 45384.

Solo:

> *Blaize,* 1989; 4 pp, 2 min.; A Minor, 4/4, "Allegro con brio" (quarter = 112); spritely, staccato triads; a legato middle section in eighths against triplets. Moderate.
>
> *Capriccios,* 1972; a suite of ten pieces.
>
> *Homage* (to William Dawson on his 90th birthday), 1990; 4 pp., 3 and 1/2 min.; starts in E Major, ends in C Major, 4/4, "Smooth flowing"; based on an African American folk song; begins slowly with the melody stated in single notes, "cantabile"; accelerates as a L.H. counter-melody joins it; freely improvisatory, with jazz harmonies. Moderate. (Published in *Black Women Composers: A Century of Piano Music,* see Appendix 1.)
>
> *Piano Potpourri,* 1980; 22 pp., 16 min.; ten pieces, ranging in difficulty from easy to moderately difficult.
>> 1. "Vignette"; 1 p.; C Major, 2/4, "Moderato (quarter = 72); lilting Scottish-style melody passes back and forth between hands; dotted rhythms. Easy.
>> 2. "Orrin and Echoe"; 1 p.; G Mixolydian, 2/4, "Andante" (quarter = 80); also Scottish folk-like quality in dotted snap rhythm; concludes with a canon on the theme. Easy.
>> 3. "Ties"; 1 p., 1 min.; G Mixolydian, 3/4 "Andante" (quarter = 92); two-voice, flowing counterpoint; folk-like quality. Easy.
>> 4. "Flight"; 3 and 1/2 pp.; E Minor, 2/4, "Presto" (quarter = 144); opens with a brilliant, rising arpeggio; a perpetual motion toccata marked "con fuoco"; motoric eighth-note patterns, hands together in parallel and contrary motion; some R.H. double thirds. Moderately difficult.
>> 5. "Jazz Notes"; 1 and 1/2 pp., 1 and 1/2 min.; G Major, 4/4, "Adagietto" (quarter = 76); melody resembles spiritual; mildly jazzy chords. Moderate.
>> 6. "Teeta"; 2 pp., 1 and 1/2 min.; B-flat Minor, 4/4 "Slow"

(quarter = 52-56); a simple, expressive melody marked "Tenderly" and one variation with a L.H. accompaniment in flowing counterpoint, marked "sempre grazioso, delicato." Easy to moderate.

7. "Promenade"; 4 pp., 2 and 1/2 min.; F Major, 4/4 "Allegro con spirito" (quarter = 120); spritely march in dotted-eighth rhythms; middle section with octave and chord leaps; key changes (E Major). Moderately difficult.

8. "Times Seven"; 6 and 1/2 pp., 4 min.; A Minor, 4/4, "Adagio"; a sombre eight measure theme and seven variations, by turns lyrical, pompous, playful, in flowing 5/4, elaborately figured, and in double octaves. Moderately difficult.

9. "Soliloquy," 1979; 3 and 1/2 pp., 4 min.; A Minor, changing meters "Moderately slow" (eighth = 72); reflective, suggests blues; a short middle section is "piu animato" with more lively, rhythmic interest.   Moderately difficult.

10. "Round and Round"; 3 pp., 1 and 1/2 min.; D Minor, 6/8, "Moderato" (quarter = 104); two-voice counterpoint; lilting, dance-like. Moderate.

Rhapsody 1964; 5 and 1/2 pp.; G Minor , 4/4, "dolce molto espressivo" (quarter = 72); begins slowly with melody in quarter-note motion, gradually increasing motion with L.H. eighth-note and triplet-eighth accompaniment; expressive, reflective, introverted, improvisatory.   Moderately difficult.

Sonata, 1968; published by Associated Composers, Inc. in 1968 (out of print).

Sonatina, 1970; 9 pp.; two movements. Moderate.

I. "Allegro"; E Minor, 3/8, (eighth = 126); cheerfully flowing legato counterpoint alternates with spritely, dance-like sections featuring L.H. octave skips in a rising chromatic sequence.

II. "Lively"; C Major/A Minor tonality (ambiguous), 2/4; rhythmic, dance-like; repeated patterns of staccato chords.

Three Impressions, 1977.

Ensemble:

Episode I and II for French Horn and Piano, 1983. Moderately difficult.

I. "Largo - Moderato"; 3 pp.; "Moderato" section in 7/8; quartal harmonies; blocks of patterns and sounds.

II. "Lively"; (quarter = 116-120); 8 pp.; B-flat tonality, mostly 5/4, (quarter = 116-120); brilliant sound, rhythmic, driving.

Excursion, violin, cello and piano (1989); 8 and 1/2 pp.; atonal, changing meters, "Andantino" (quarter = 68-70); opens without piano: violin and cello interchange of rhapsodic flourishes; contrapuntal middle section with more regular motion; pizzicato transition back to rhapsodic material of the opening.

Fantasy, violin and piano, n.d.; 8 and 1/2 pp.; F-sharp Minor (freely shifting tonalities), 4/4 (some meter changes); opens with solo violin flourish marked "Intenso" (quarter = 144); continues "Moderato" (quarter = 100-120) in contrapuntal duet with piano; middle section "molto piu tranquillo" (quarter = 92) becoming "piu agitato"; closing section brings back and extends the rhapsodic violin flourishes of the opening. Moderately difficult.

Four Mynyms for Three Players, flute, oboe and piano, 1968; 11 pp., 5 min.; both name and music suggest miniatures, medieval minstrels; linear counterpoint; mildly dissonant. Moderately difficult.
   1. "Pensive"; modal, 3/8, "Moderato" (eighth = 112-116); three independent, interweaving melodic lines.
   2. "Jovial"; pentatonic, 2/4, "Lively" (quarter = 126-132); gapped scales give a primitive, folk-like quality to this movement; middle section in 5/8.
   3. "Melancholy"; E-flat Major, 4/4, "Slow" (quarter = 60); imitative counterpoint.
   4. "Jubilant"; D Minor, 4/4, "Fast" (quarter = 152-156); rhythmic, dance-like; features a duet for flute and oboe, and a solo for piano.

Sonatine, clarinet and piano, 1969; 16 pp.; in three movements. Moderately difficult.
   I. "Fast"; (quarter = 92-120); bold, assertive piano opening; the two instruments in both parallel and independent melodic motion in eighths and sixteenths
   II. "Moderately slow"; A Minor, 2/4, "espressivo" (quarter = 80-88); clarinet cantilena over slow, steady piano motion.
   III. "Rather Lively (scherzando)"; A Minor, 3/4, (dotted half = 112-124); ternary form; piano opens with rhythmic dance; clarinet enters with scalar melodic line in eighths; shift to more rapidly moving middle section in 6/8 (dotted quarter = 128); return to opening section: this

time the clarinet takes some of the piano's melodic material.

Two Letters, clarinet, cello and piano, 1975. Moderately difficult.

> 1) "(Written in Spring)"; E Major, 2/4 "Gaily but not too fast" (quarter = 112); cheerful, freshly innocent melodies.
>
> 2) "(Written at Summer's End)"; E Major, 4/4, "Moderately slow" (quarter = 66-72); reflective, nostalgic, improvisatory effect.

(Composer, Anderson, Cohen, Holly, Southall)

Price, Florence Beatrice, née Smith

b. 9 April 1887 in Little Rock, Arkansas; d. 3 June 1953 in Chicago, Illinois. Pianist, organist, teacher, and composer. Her father was Dr. James H. Smith, a dentist and inventor, and her mother, Florence Irene Gulliver, was an elementary school teacher. The first black woman to win recognition as a composer in the United States, Price was educated in the segregated public schools of Little Rock, Arkansas. One of her instructors was Charlotte Andrews Stephens, a gifted teacher whose students also included William Grant Still. She went on to Little Rock's Capitol High School from which she graduated as valedictorian of her class in 1903. Price received her early music training from her mother who presented her in a recital of her own works at age four. She was enrolled in the New England Conservatory of Music in Boston in 1903 and graduated in 1906 with a diploma in organ and piano pedagogy. She then returned to Arkansas to teach at the Cotton Plant Arkadelphia Academy and Shorter College (1906–1910), and at Clark University in Atlanta, GA (1910–1912). In 1912 she returned to Little Rock to marry an attorney, Thomas J. Price. They had a son, Tommy, who died in infancy (the song "To My Little Son" was written in his memory), and two daughters, Florence Louise and Edith. In 1926, the family moved to Chicago because of increasing racial violence in Little Rock. Florence Price continued studies at several Chicago institutions: Chicago Musical College, American Conservatory, Chicago Teachers' College, Central YMCA College, and the University of Chicago. Her works won a number of prizes including the Casper Holstein prize in 1926 for *In the Land O'Cotton* and in 1927 for *Memories of Dixieland,* and the Rodman Wanamaker prize for her *Symphony in E Minor* in 1932, the same year her piano *Sonata in E Minor* and *Fantasie no. 4* also won

Wanamaker prizes. This competition brought her to the attention of Frederick Stock, who conducted the Chicago Symphony Orchestra in a performance of her *Symphony in E Minor* at the World's Fair in 1933. She was one of the pioneer black symphonists, along with William Grant Still and William Dawson, and her many orchestral works received performances by the Chicago Symphony Orchestra, Chicago Women's Symphony, Detroit Symphony, Michigan WPA Symphony, American Symphony, Brooklyn and Bronx Symphonies, Pittsburgh Symphony and as far away as England, where Sir John Barbirolli commissioned a work for the Manchester Symphony Orchestra. Her music reflects her classical training as well as the influence of Antonin Dvořák, the Bohemian nationalist composer who urged American composers to exploit their own native music, particularly Negro folk song and spirituals. She was able to blend European techniques with idioms developed from African traditions. These included melodies based on the gapped scale, call and response forms, and syncopated rhythms derived from the cakewalk and the juba, produced by foot stamping on the beat alternately with hand clapping or patting off the beat. Her spiritual arrangements and art songs were widely performed by many celebrated singers, most notably Marian Anderson and Roland Hayes. She was active in the Chicago Club of Women Organists, and her organ music was also frequently performed. Some of it was published, along with many songs and piano teaching pieces, by the McKinley, G. Schirmer, Theodore Presser, Galaxy, Carl Fischer, Clayton F. Summy, and Lorenz publishing companies. Today most of her pieces are out of print and her large works remain in manuscript. Her approximately 300 compositions encompass almost every form and genre, including radio commercials and popular songs (under the name Vee Jay). In 1964, more than a decade after her death, one of Chicago's new elementary schools was named after her, and at the dedication program (which included her *Violin Concerto no. 2*) the second grade students performed songs by her from the Silver Burdett public school music series. Many of her manuscripts, letters, and other memorabilia were left by her daughter, Florence Price Robinson, to the University of Arkansas, where a list of holdings and copies of works may be obtained through Special Collections, University of Arkansas Libraries, Fayetteville, AR 72701. Music listed below which is from that collection is marked U. of A. Some teaching pieces are available from the Chicago Public Library, Fine Arts Division, 78 East Washington Street, Chicago, Illinois 60605 (indicated by ChicPL). The locations of other works, where known, are indicated.

Solo:

Anticipation, c. 1928, published by McKinley. Grade II.

Arkansas Jitter, 1938, ms.; 4 pp.; C Major, 2/4, "Allegretto" (quarter = 138); oddly syncopated dance with stops and catches created by ties; chromatic; ternary form, with middle section in A minor. Moderate. (U. of A.)

At the Cotton Gin, A Southern Sketch for Piano, c. 1927, published by G. Schirmer in 1927; took a prize in the 1926 Casper Holstein contest, according to her daughter, Florence Price Robinson, this piece "was entered in a contest by her husband without her knowledge and won a cash award, publication and a royalty contract"; 4 pp.; A-flat Major, 2/4, "Allegro"; unhurried, cheerful melody over steady eighth accompaniment (divided between hands), like a cotton gin machine; momentary "lapses" into E Major give the effect of a change in pitch of machine hum; R.H. plays both melody and its share of accompaniment; double notes; middle section in E Major has similar "lapses" into C Major. Moderate. (U. of A.)

Bayou Dance, 1938, ms.; 3 pp.; A-flat Major, 2/4, "Tempo moderato"; jaunty, syncopated melody over steady L.H. quarter note accompaniment, features a bass line which rises a half-step each measure, from A-flat to D; ternary form, with middle section in C Minor. Moderate. (U. of A.)

Birds in the Forest, n.d.; published by McKinley. Grade II.

Blue Skies, n.d.; published by McKinley. Grade II.

The Bridle Path

"Bright Eyes," see *Three Sketches for Little Pianists.*

*The Butterfly,*c. 1936, published by Carl Fischer in *Pieces We Like to Play;* 3 pp.; G major, 6/8, "Brightly"; teaching piece with commentary on three-part form and suggestions for alternate fingerings; two-note slurred accompaniment; some double fourths; pedal carefully marked; ternary form with middle section in C major and melody shifting to L.H. Easy to moderate. (ChicPL)

"Cabin Song,"see *Three Sketches for Little Pianists*

Clover Blossom, published by McKinley in 1947.

The Cotton Dance, 1931, published by Oxford University Press in *Oxford Piano Course,* Book Five, in 1942; won Honorable Mention in Wanamaker contest, 1931; 3 pp.; F Major, 2/4, "Allegretto"; teaching piece with commentary on five-part rondo form; jaunty, syncopated; momentary shifts in and out of A-flat major. Moderate. (U. of A.)

Criss Cross, c. 1947; published by McKinley.

Dainty Feet

Dance of the Cotton Blossoms, 1938, ms.; 3 pp.; G Major, 2/4, "Allegretto"; syncopated dance; rapid leaps; chromatic; middle section in E-flat Major. Moderate. (U. of A.)

Dances in the Canebrakes, "based on authentic Negro rhythms," c. 1953, published by Affiliated Musicians/ Mills Music, Los Angeles, 1953; three pieces. (U. of A.)

1. "Nimble Feet"; 3 pp.; E Major, 4/8, "Allegro"; syncopated theme in middle, played by L.H. over bass half note down-beats; R.H. chords off-beat, juba-style; rapid hand crossing; ternary form with middle section in E Minor and new theme also in L.H. with R.H. maintaining off-beats; on return, first theme spreads out with alternate phrases in high register octaves, in call and response. Moderate.

2. "Tropical Noon"; 4. pp.; A Major, 4/8, "Andantino"; leisurely melody; juba-style rhythmic pattern between hands; ternary form with middle section in D Minor, low register. Moderate.

3. "Silk Hat and Walking Cane"; 4 pp.; F Major, 2/4, "Moderato"; steady eighth L.H. accompaniment and cheerful, syncopated R.H. melody starting in high register and making its way down the keyboard; ternary form with middle section in D Minor. Moderate.

Dark Path

Doll Waltz, c. 1928; published by McKinley.Grade II.

Echoes, n.d.; published by McKinley. Grade II.

An Elf on a Moonbeam

The Engine, c.1928; published by McKinley.Grade II.

Evening, n.d.; published by McKinley.Grade II.

Fantasie Negre, 1929, ms.; dedicated "To my talented little friend, Margaret A. Bonds,"; Price's most ambitious work for piano located to date, next to her *Sonata in E Minor;* 9 pp.; E Minor, 4/4, "Andante"; combines ternary and variation forms in florid fantasia-style; sixteen-measure introduction employing motives from the theme which follows, the spiritual, "Sinner, Please Don't Let This Harvest Pass" (unusual instance of actual quote in Price's music); theme presented in several highly contrapuntal, chromatic variations, interspersed with improvisatory, virtuoso passage-work; B section is a short, contrasting, folk lullaby in G Major, marked"Andante cantabile"; return to spiritual theme in more variations alternating with modulatory passage-work; dramatic, bravura ending.

Difficult. (Copies of the manuscript located at the Library of Congress and the Marian Anderson Collection, University of Pennsylvania Van Pelt Library; published in *Black Women Composers: A Century of Piano Music.*)

Fantasie Negre no. 4 in B Minor for Piano, 1932, possibly the one which won Honorable Mention in the Wanamaker contest that year; it received its first Chicago performance by Marion Hall at a WPA Composers Forum concert on 15 June 1937 (Holly).

The Flame, n.d.; ms. owned by Florence M. Stith, also in private Frederick D. Hall Collection.

The Gnat and the Bee, c. 1936; published by Carl Fischer in *Pieces We like to Play;* 3 pp.; C Major, 4/4, "Fast and Vigorous"; teaching piece with commentary on three-part form; starts with melody passed back and forth between the hands; syncopated L.H. accompaniment; L.H. grace notes; ends with glissando. Easy. (ChicPL)

The Goblin and the Mosquito, c. 1951, published by Clayton F. Summy; 2 pp.; A Minor, 4/8, "Allegro" (quarter = 112); features quickly alternating hands, juba-style; rapid groups of grace notes. Easy to moderate. (U. of A.)

Here and There, c. 1947; published by McKinley.

Hiking, n.d.; published by McKinley. Grade II.

"Hoe Cake," see *Three Little Negro Dances.*

In the Land O' Cotton, Holstein Second Prize, 1926.

Joy in June

Lake Mirror, n.d.; ms. owned by Florence M. Stith and also in the private Frederick D. Hall Collection.

Levee Dance, c. 1937, published by T. Presser; 5 pp.; G Major, 4/8, "Allegro" (quarter = 116); ternary AbA C A form in which the A section has its own middle section, a juba rhythm divided between the hands; middle section in C Major with new juba-type material. Moderate. (ChicPL)

March of the Beetles, c. 1947; published by McKinley.

Mellow Twilight, published by T.Presser in 1929; Grade III; also arranged for violin and piano.

Memories of Dixieland, Holstein Second Prize, 1927.

Moon Behind a Cloud, n.d.; ms. owned by Florence M. Stith and also in the Frederick D. Hall Collection.

"Morning Sunbeam," see *Three Sketches for Little Pianists.*

Nimble Feet, see *Dances in the Canebrakes.*

Nobody Knows the Trouble I See, published by T. Presser, 1938.

The Old Boatman, c. 1951, published by Clayton F. Summy; 2 pp.; G major, 4/4, "Andante" (half note = 126); quiet, poignant melody accompanied by rocking motive; hands switch roles; pedal carefully marked; ternary form. **Easy.** (U. of A.)

On Parade, n.d.; published by McKinley. Grade II.

On Top of a Tree

Pensive Mood

A Photograph, n.d.; published by Carl Fischer. Grade II.

"Rabbit Foot"; see *Three Little Negro Dances.*

Rock a Bye, c. 1947; published by McKinley.

Rocking Chair, 1939; ms.; 2 pp.; E-flat Major, 6/8, "Allegretto"; gently rocking accompaniment; soothing melody in long notes; occasional use of flatted sevenths and thirds; shifts of key to G Major, and G-flat Major. Moderate. (U. of A.)

The Rose, c. 1936, published by Carl Fischer; as part of *Pieces We Like to Play;* 2 pp.; F Major, 3/4, "Moderato cantando"; teaching piece with commentary on three-part form; hands switch roles, legato and staccato. Easy. (ChicPL)

A Sachem's Pipe, c. 1935, published by Carl Fischer in *Pieces We Like to Play;* 2 pp.; F-sharp Minor, 4/4, "With dignity"; teaching piece with commentary on three-part form, and quote from Longfellow's "The Song of Hiawatha": "From his pouch he drew his peace-pipe . . ."; steady L.H. open fifths set drum-beat pattern; large skips; L.H. melody crossed hands. Easy to moderate. (ChicPL)

The Sea Swallow, c. 1951, published by Clayton F. Summy; 2 pp.; C major, 2/2, "Andantino"; teaching piece; exercise in crossing hands and pedal; rarely hands together. Very easy. (U. of A.)

"Silk Hat and Walking Cane"; see *Dances in the Canebrakes.*

Sonata in E Minor, 1932, ms.; took First Prize in Wanamaker Contest, 1932; Price's most ambitious work for piano; three movements; 27 pp., 25 min. Difficult. (Manuscript located at the Library of Congress.)

    I. "Andante - Allegro"; 4/4 - 2/4, E Minor; classical sonata-allegro form; introductory heroic opening statement; exposition with two main themes, the second marked "Allegretto"; concludes in G Major; development veers to B Minor, includes augmentation of theme no. 1 in the bass, and its inversion in the treble; recapitulation returns to E Minor; themes grow in poignany as they return in minor key.

    II. "Andante"; C Major, 4/8; lyrical, contrapuntal; folk-like melody with characteristic gap of third; slow, pensive cakewalk rhythm; rondo form with two episodes.

III. "Scherzo: Allegro"; E Minor, 6/8; lengthy parody of European concert music; sections in the styles of Tchaikovsky and Rachmaninoff juxtaposed with cakewalks, extravagant Broadway-style build-ups; two main sections: the first in ternary form consisting of a motoric theme treated in virtuoso style and a middle passage of romantic Rachmaninoff-style melody and accompaniment; the second, a rondo with rollicking refrain and cakewalk episodes; exuberant virtuoso ending.

Swaying Buttercups, n.d.; published by McKinley. Grade II.

The Swing, n.d., published by McKinley. Grade II.

Tecumseh, c. 1935; published by Carl Fischer in *Pieces We Like to Play*. Grade III.

Three Boughs, n.d.; published by McKinley. Grade II.

Three Little Negro Dances, c. 1933, published by T. Presser; best-known of Price's easy teaching sets; "Ticklin' Toes" still in print; also arranged and published for band; performed by the United States Marine Band. (ChicPL)

1. "Hoe Cake"; 3 pp.; C major, 4/8, "Allegro" (quarter = 132); syncopated R.H. against a steady L.H.; some melody plus accompaniment in R.H.; grace notes; L.H. accompaniment in double thirds, fourths; hands switch roles. Easy to moderate.

2. "Rabbit Foot"; 2 pp.; F Major, 4/8, "Allegretto" (quarter = 120); many grace notes; double notes. Easy to moderate.

3. "Ticklin' Toes"; 4 pp.; C Major, 4/8, "Allegro molto" (quarter = 138); syncopated R.H. against steady L.H., with some juba-style rhythmic alternation of hands; grace notes; ternary form. Easy to moderate.

"Ticklin' Toes," c. 1933; see *Three Little Negro Dances*.

Three Sketches for Little Pianists, c. 1937, published by T. Presser. (Two of the three located at ChicPL.)

1. "Cabin Song"; 2 pp.; F Major, 2/2, "Moderato" (half note = 88); alternating hands; legato slurs. Very easy.

2. "Bright Eyes,"C Major, 6/8, "Allegretto" (quarter = 92); few shifts; alternating hands; both legato slurs and staccato. Very easy.

3. "A Morning Sunbeam"

"Tropical Noon"; see *Dances in the Canebrakes*.

Undecided

TheWaltzing Fairy, c. 1928, published by McKinley; 3 pp.; C Major, 3/4, "Valse Allegretto" (half note = 69); teaching piece with commentary on motives; hands together;

changes from legato to staccato. Easy. (U.of A.)

The Waterfall, c. 1937, published by McKinley in 1928. Easy.

A Wee Bit of Erin

Were You there When They Crucified My Lord? published by Oxford U. Press in *Oxford Piano Course,* Book Five, in 1942; 2 pp.; C Major, 4/4, "Andante"; solo piano setting of the spiritual; teaching piece with commentary on spirituals and form; chord analysis; simple hymn-style; pedal marked. Easy to moderate. (U. of A.)

Who Will Dance with Me?, n.d.; published by McKinley, Grade II.

The Zephry, Mexican folk song transcribed for piano solo; published by McKinley in 1938.

In addition, there are numerous very easy teaching pieces, some available from the University of Arkansas in negative photocopy; "Autumn Echoes," "Brownies at the Seashore," "Brung, the Bear," "Climbing the Mountain," "The Froggie and the Rabbit," "Golden Corn Tassels," "Little Pieces on Black Keys, " "Little Pieces on White Keys," "The Moo-cow, Fido, and Kitty," "Nodding Poppies," "On Higher Ground," "On the Playground," "A Pleasant Thought," "Strong Men Forward," "Up and Down the Ladder." A more complete list is in Brown, the source of the unlocated items on this list.

Ensemble:

Annie Laurie, two pianos/four hands, n.d., published by McKinley.

By Candlelight, violin and piano, published by McKinley.

Concerto for Piano and Orchestra in One Movement, D Minor, 1934; also in two piano version; mss. owned by Rae Linda Brown and also in Frederick D. Hall Collection.

The Deserted Garden, violin and piano, 1933, published by Theodore Presser; 2 pp.; D Minor, 4/4, "Andante con espressione"; pensive melody; simple counterpoint in accompaniment. Easy to moderate. (U. of A.)

Elfentanz, violin and piano, n.d.,ms.; dedicated to Alan Lane, Chicago violinist; 6 pp.; D major. 2/4, "Allegretto moderato"; spritely piece in ternary form with contrasting "Andante" middle section in B-flat Major; sharing of melodic motives. Moderate. (U. of A.)

Fantasie Negre, two pianos/four hands; n.d.; it was played by the composer and another pianist for Katherine Dunham's dance interpretation.

"Hoe Cake," two pianos/four hands, c.1949, arranged from

Three Little Negro Dances (see solos above) and published by T. Presser; each part more difficult than solo version: octave doubling, more sixteenth note passages. Moderately difficult. (U. of A.)

Mellow Twilight, violin and piano, 1930, published by Theodore Presser.

Playful Rondo, violin and piano, published by McKinley.

Quintet in E Minor, piano and strings,1936; performed by the Forum Quartet with pianist Marion Hall at a Chicago WPA concert on 15 June 1937 (Holly).
1. "Allegro ma non troppo"
2. "Andante con moto"
3. "Juba"
4. "Scherzo"

"Rabbit Foot," two pianos/four hands, 1949, published by T. Presser.

Rhapsody for piano and orchestra

Silent Night, two pianos/four hands, n.d., published by McKinley.

Sonatine, for cello and piano

Suite for Brasses and Piano

Three Little Negro Dances, two pianos/four hands, c. 1949, published by T. Presser; see **Hoe Cake,** above.

"Ticklin' Toes," two pianos/four hands, c. 1949, published by T Presser; see *Three Little Negro Dances,* above.

Two Moods, flute, clarinet and piano, 1953, performed by the Clara Siegel Chamber Players in 1953 in Illinois.

Selected Bibliography:

Brown, Rae Linda. List of Works by Florence Price. Unpublished, n.d.

———. "The Orchestral Works of Florence B. Price (1888-1953): A Stylistic Analysis." Ph.D. diss., Yale University, 1987.

Holly, Ellistine Perkins. "Black Concert Music in Chicago, 1890 to the 1930s."*Black Music Research Newsletter* 9, no. 2 (Fall 1987):3–7.

Green, Mildred Denby. "Florence Price." Chap. 2 in *Black Women Composers: A Genesis.* Boston: Twayne Publishers, 1983.

Jackson, Barbara Garvey. "Florence Price, Composer." *Black Perspective in Music* 7, no. 1 (Spring 1977):30-43.

Patterson, Willis. *Anthology of Art Songs by Black American Composers.* New York: E. B. Marks, 1977.

Sizer, Sam. "A Checklist of Source Materials By and About Florence B. Price." University of Arkansas Library. Special Collections Division, 1977.

(Abdul, Ammer, ASCAP, Block, BrownJWJ, Carter, Cohen, Hare,

Holly, Meggett, NegYB1952, NGrDAM, Roach, SouBD, SouMBA, Williams, etc.)

Ramos-Harris, Ethel, see Harris, Ethel Ramos

Richardson, Victoria

b. late-nineteenth century. Composer. Listed in the Walter Whittlesey File at the Library of Congress with two published works, neither in the LC holdings. One of them, a vocal quartet, "My Livingston" was published in Goldsboro, North Carolina in 1901, copyright number C 7722. The other is the piano piece listed below.

Solo:
   The Mountain Stream, for piano, n.d.

(LCWh)

Ricketts, Estelle D.

b. late-nineteenth century. Composer. According to the copyright card, she resided in Darby, Pennsylvania in 1893. She is listed as a composer, Miss Estelle Rickets (sic), on page 27 of Mrs. N. F. Mossell's *The Work of the Afro-American Woman* (Philadelphia, 1894). She may be the Stella D. Rickets listed in the 1900 U.S. Census Records as black, born in July 1871 in Pennsylvania and living with her parents and younger brother at 115 10th Street in Darby, Pennsylvania, where her father operated a boarding stable.

Solo:
   Rippling Spring Waltz, c. 1893, published (n.p.) by E. D. Ricketts; 4 pp.; G Major, 3/4; multi-sectioned, mostly eight or sixteen measures long; each has a new melody, although several seem related to the descending line of the first melody; it returns in its original form near the end. Moderate. (Copies available through Library of Congress, copyright number 8638; published in *Black Women Composers: A Century of Piano Music,* see Appendix 1.)

(Mossell, LC copyright card)

Roberts, Josie Wilhelmina

b. late-nineteenth century. Listed in the Walter Whittlesey File of Black Musicians at the Library of Congress with one published composition (located in their holdings and listed below), and no other information.

Solo:

Talladega March, c. 1905 by J. W. Roberts and published by the composer, n.p.; may possibly have been a piano score for a band piece, since small additional inner notes are inserted at times; 3 pp.; B-flat major, 6/8, no indication; over-all form is binary, with a ternary "Trio" but no da capo return; a four measure introduction, followed by a sixteen measure A section marked *p* with second ending: R.H. melody in octaves and standard L.H. accompaniment leaping between a bass octave doubled root to chord in middle register; another sixteen measure section B, marked *ff* with new melody, also in R.H. octaves and similar L.H. accompaniment; the "Trio" is in E-flat Major; first section is almost the same as opening A section, marked *mf,* with varied L.H. octave line; the second Trio section is a more brilliant alternation between a four note bass motive and echoing treble four note motive, followed by a L.H. octave melody which builds to the conclusion without a second ending (eighteen measures in all); it concludes with a repetition of the Trio's first section with second ending, this time marked *ff;* it has the effect of a da capo return because of the resemblance to the opening section. Moderately difficult (lots of octaves, both hands). (Copy in the Library of Congress, call number M28.R.)

(LCWh)

Robinson, Gertrude Rivers

b. 30 June 1927 in Washington, D.C. Ethnomusicologist, educator, gamelan performer, and composer. Robinson received her B.A. in performance and composition from Cornell University, where she studied with Robert Palmer. Her M.A. is from the University of California at Los Angeles and her teachers there were Roy Harris, Colin McPhee and Boris Kremenliev. Her studies in ethnomusicology led to her thesis composition, *Bayangan for Western Septet, Balinese Octet, Dancer and Visuals.* which has been performed in

Los Angeles, San Diego, and Mexico City. She has a Candidate for Ph.D. degree from the University of California at Los Angeles and has specialized in the music of Indonesia and Africa, traveling widely on field trips. She served as musical director and teacher for the Lester Horton Dance Theater, and also taught at Cornell University. She was the founder of the Stark Studios of Music, Dance and Arts in Palms, California. Since 1970, she has been on the music faculty of Loyola Marymount University in Los Angeles. She is founder/ director of the ILMU Gamelan Society and has served on numerous panels including the Music Panel of the National Endowment for the Arts. She has a number of publications to her credit and played the lead gamelan instrument in the Columbia Masterworks recording *The Exotic Sounds of Bali* as well as the Institute of Ethnomusicology recording *Music of the Venerable Dark Cloud* under the direction of Mantle Hood. Her works include several scores for the Lester Horton Dance Theater and dancers Alvin Ailey, Eugene Loring, and Gloria Newman, as well as a *Trio* (1949) for clarinet, violin, and cello, and *Sleep*, for voice and piano, on a text of William Shakespeare, performed by Sheila Tate in May/ June 1989 at the Manhattan School of Music, New York, and Loyola Marymount Murphy Hall, Los Angeles. Her unpublished works may be requested from her at her address: 4549 Circle View Blvd., Los Angeles, CA 90043.

Solo:

> *Cry*, 1948, composed at Cornell University, Ithaca, New York for choreography by Helvi Selkee, danced by May Atherton; performed 17 March 1991 by pianist Althea Waites at Sherman Clay Hall, Los Angeles, and 20 May 1991 at California State Polytechnic University in Pomona, California; inspired by the poem, "Murder at Lidice" by Edna St. Vincent Millay: "First came Spring, with planting and sowing, Then came summer, with haying and hoeing . . . Then came quiet and nothing more . . . Hear us when we speak; oh hear what we say . . ."; 6 pp.; A Minor, 3/4, "Andante tranquillo"; sets atmosphere for dramatic modern dance; three episodes depict scenes of St. Vincent Millay's poem; opens with mournful four-note melodic motive repeated slowly like an incantation, under an accompaniment of repeated triplet major seconds; sudden change of meter and tempo indication to 3/8 "Allegro"; second episode in 5/4 "Largo" and third in 4/4; ritualistic repetition of other melodic motives; drum beats between episodes one and two simulated by strumming on bass strings

inside piano. Moderate.

Sketches , 1951, for children's classes in modern dance.

Ensemble:

Moods I and II, flute and piano, 1986, published in "A Festschrift presented to J. H. Kwabena Nketia." *African Musicology: Current Trends* 1 (1989): 321— (Crossroads Press/ African Studies Association, University of California, Los Angeles); according to the composer, these pieces reflect the influence of Japanese painting and non-Western performance practices; 10 pp.   Moderately difficult.

I. "Andante"; 4 pp.; no key signature, changing meters, (quarter = 60); "designed for choreography, inspired by the letters of Narcissa Whitman, an American pioneer woman"; meditative and impressionistic; opens with recitative for solo flute; piano has a long, lyrical solo section, widely spaced quartal and quintal harmonies, open sound.

II. "Allegro scherzando"; 6 pp.; no key signature, 3/4, (quarter = 190); composer's comment: "an additional layer for guitar is to be improvised in the manner of the West African drummer"; spirited, playful, dance-like; parallel major sevenths, fourths; melody with repeated motives.

Moods, soprano saxophone and piano, available on Cambria recording (see Discography); same as *Moods I and II* for flute, transposed down a major second in *Mood II*.

Quintet for Piano and Strings, 1950.

Seven Scenes with Balabil, two pianos, 1952, for Lester Horton.

Dedication to Ruth, Mary, Martha, flute and piano, 1952, for Lester Horton.

Dedication to Carson McCullers, flute and piano, 1953, for Lester Horton.

(Composer, Southall)

Schuyler, Philippa Duke

b. 2 August 1931 in New York City; d. 9 May 1967 in Danang, South Vietnam.   Pianist, composer, and author.   A child prodigy, Schuyler began her public concert career at age four, when she was already composing little piano pieces.   Her father was George

Schuyler, an author and editor of the *Pittsburgh Courier*, and her mother was Josephine Codgell, a wealthy Texas heiress. When she was twelve years old, Philippa's award-winning composition, *Manhattan Nocturne*, was performed by the Detroit Symphony Orchestra as well as the New York Philharmonic Orchestra. At fourteen, she made her piano debut with the New York Philharmonic, playing with the Boston Symphony the same year. She made her Town Hall debut in 1953 to rave reviews, and in later years, she made three world tours under the auspices of the State Department, as well as numerous guest soloist and composer appearances with orchestras in the United States and abroad. She was also an author and news correspondent for the *Manchester Union-Leader* (N.H.). Her books include *Adventures in Black and White* (Foreword by Deems Taylor, New York: Robert Speller and Sons, 1960), *Jungle Saints, Africa's Heroic Catholic Missionaries* (Rome: Herder and Herder, 1963), *Who Killed the Congo?* (New York, Devin Adair Company, 1962) and *Good Men Die*, (New York: Twin Circle Publishers, 1969). She died in a U.S. Army helicopter crash while evacuating Vietnamese children from Hue to Danang. She was on assignment in Vietnam as a correspondent. Her approximately sixty compositions, many of them incomplete, are primarily for piano, although she also wrote orchestral and vocal music. They are characteristically autobiographical and programmatic, conservative in form, yet revealing her love of Africa and of occult numeric and intervallic codes. Most of the manuscript scores may be seen at the Schomburg Center for Research in Black Culture in New York City and others are at the Library of Congress. Memorabilia and recordings are also housed at the Indiana University School of Music Library. Other sources for individual scores are indicated below.

Solo:
>   Many juvenile pieces in pencil manuscript including a *Cockroach Ballet, Suite from the Arabian Nights,* and *Dance of the Forty Thieves,* composed at age six. Also early printed music:
>   *Three Little Pieces,* c. 1938, published by Mrs. George Schuyler (her mother). See *Nine Little Pieces,* below. (Copies available from the James Weldon Johnson Memorial Collection. Beinecke Rare Books and Manuscript Library, Yale University Library, Box 1603A Yale Station, New Haven, CT 06520.)
>   1. "The Wolf"
>   2. "Autumn Rain"

3. "The Jolly Pig"

Five Little Pieces, c. 1938; the same, plus

    4. "At the Circus"

    5. "Farewell"

Eight Little Pieces, c. 1938; the same, plus

    6. "Men at Work (The WPA on a Construction Site)"

    7. "Morning Miniature"

    8. "Postscript"

Nine Little Pieces, c. 1938, the same as *Eight Little Pieces* plus "Song of the Machine." Easy. (Copies also available from the James Weldon Johnson Collection, see address above.)

1. "The Wolf"; 1/2 p.; C Major, 2/4, "Moderato"; triads repeated in each octave of keyboard from two octaves below middle C to two octaves above; shows Philippa's love of repeated patterns and sequences.

2. "Autumn Rain"; 1 p.; C major, 3/8, "Allegretto"; broken triads repeated, hand over hand, in each octave from low to high; light, staccato two-note repeated patterns in high and low registers, simulating rain.

3. "The Jolly Pig"; 1/2 p.; D Major, 2/4, "Allegro con moto"; R.H. and L.H. take turns playing two-note phrases against Alberti bass; R.H. descending scales; lots of repetition.

4. "At the Circus"; 1 and 1/2 pp.; C Major; several sections in different meters and patterns; opens with a march-like introduction in 4/4; next section in 3/4 repeats same two-note phrase in R.H. over L.H. waltz accompaniment in shifting harmonies; third section in A Minor, 4/4, features repeated motives over broken fifths; da capo, with coda.

5. "Farewell"; 1/2 p.; A Minor, 4/4, no tempo indication; R.H. melody begins with octave leap, contrasts regular and off-beat rhythmic patterns; L.H. triad accompaniment.

6. "Men at Work," subtitled "The WPA on a construction job"; 2 pp.; no key signature (atonal), 8/8, "Allegro con fuoco"; repetition of imitative sound effects: crashing chords, motoristic activity in thirty-second notes; L.H. broken octaves.

7. "Song of the Machine (in a defense factory)"; 1/2 p.; A Minor, 4/4; repetition of motoristic patterns, dissonant quartal harmonies.

8. "Morning Miniature"; 1/2 p.; A Major, 4/4, "Allegro moderato"; melody and accompaniment with a bit of counterpoint; quiet, tonal, and gracefully proportioned.

9. "Postscript"; 1/2 p.; D Minor, 3/4, "Allegro risoluto"; quirky
   melody with rapid, repeated oom-pah accompaniment in
   eighths.

Adult works:

African Rhapsody, 1964; no score; tape available at Indiana
   University Music Library; premiered December, 1964 at
   United Nations Embassy in Togo, Africa.

Ben Hashim, ca. 1958; 21 pp.; part of the White Nile Suite, see
   below.

Khanghai, 1959; 3 pp.; composed during first trip to Hong Kong
   in 1959.

Nubian Legend, 1965, no score; tape may be heard at Indiana
   University Music Library.

The Rhapsody of Youth, 1950; no score.; premiered in 1950 in
   Haiti.

Rumpelstiltsken, **piano arrangement of an orchestral piece
   composed in 1944-1945, c. 1955 by publisher, Ricordi
   Americana S. A. in Buenos Aires; 10 pp.; F Minor, 12/8,
   "Molto allegro scherzoso" (dotted quarter = 138-152);
   brilliant perpetual motion in A B A B A form; L.H. eighths
   against R.H. staccato chords, also together in parallel
   motion; middle section "cantate piu *p* e molto legato" with
   sustained R.H. melody over syncopated repeated-note bass;
   repeated in different registers, doublings, chords, accompa-
   niments, with indications suggesting different instrumental
   imitation ("come trompetas," etc.). Moderately difficult.
   (Copy at the JWJ Collection, see above.)**

Scherzo Parisien, ca. 1966; ms.; 4 pp.; premiered in 1966.

The Seven Pillars of Wisdom, piano and narrator, 1958; ms.; 38
   pp.; Prologue, seven movements and Epilogue; text from T.E.
   Lawrence, *Seven Pillars of Wisdom*, precedes each movement.

Suite Africaine, 1958; ms.; 8 pp.; three movements:
   1. "Tweyanze: Chisamnaru"
   2. "Nogomo Fumita"
   3. "Embogo Sanga"

Ummdurman, ca.1958; 21 pp.

Wanchai Road, ca. 1959; 2 pp.; place in Hong Kong where
   journalist resided, with whom Schuyler corresponded.

*White Nile Suite , A Musical Saga depicting Arab History in
   Egypt and the Sudan,* **1964; four movements, reflecting the
   influence of her African travels beginning in 1958, employing African idioms: gapped scales and intervals, meter
   changes, driving bass rhythmic patterns, timbres of African**

instruments and vocal styles. Moderately difficult. (Ms. can be seen in Library of Congress, call number ML 96.S417 No.1 Case.; movement published in *Black Women Composers: A Century of Piano Music,* see Appendix 1.)

1. "The Foundations of the Arab Revolt: The Clashing Jealousies"; 4 pp.; no key or time signature, "Allegro" (quarter = 116); imitates African/ Arabian music: exotic scales and augmented intervals; repetitive, heavily ornamented melodies over repeated L.H. accompaniment patterns; middle section features similar melodies in counterpoint; crashing chords and forearm clusters; closes with a melismatic flourish, fading away.

2. "Alexandria (oldest metropolis of modern Egypt)"; 2 pp.; oriental scale, 2/2, "Allegro ritmico" (half note = 100-120); opens with rapid, syncopated rhythmic ostinato on E-flat in bass, continued throughout piece with periodic shifts in pattern and pitch; melody in long notes ornamented with swirls of grace notes; additive rhythmic patterns.

3. "Fortune Favored the Bold Player (The Arab expansion was based on courage and faith)"; 1 and 1/2 pp.; 4/4, "Vivace" (quarter = 132); melody in short, terse, articulated phrases, accompanied by a four-note, quarter note pattern with grace groups between them simulating slide from one to the next; middle section changes to chordal two-measure phrases; returns to opening melody, retaining accompaniment pattern of middle section.

4. "The Fall of the Fortress of Babylon, Egypt (Thus began the epic of Arab-African History)"; 4 pp.; opens with an introductory section titled "Port Said" and marked "Allegro molto ritmico e rubato," a rapid and complicated rhythmic pattern in 6/8 ending in a series of descending trills; the fourth movement itself is in 4/4 and opens with a L.H. ostinato of ninths in half notes; a chain of melodic motives, each repeated for several measures, accelerates to the end.

Ensemble:

Nile Fantasia, piano and orchestra, ca. 1958; 45 pp.; four movements:

1. "The Rebellion"
2. "Inshallah"

3. "The Terror"
4. "The Road to Victory"

Selected Bibliography:
"Philippa Duke Schuyler, Pianist, Dies in Crash of a Copter in
    Vietnam " *New York Times* (10 May 1967):1.
Talalay, Kathryn. "Philippa Duke Schuyler, Pianist/ Composer/
    Writer." *Black Perspective in Music* 9, no. 1 (Spring 1982):43–68.
(ASCAP, Carter, Cohen, Holly, NegYB1952, SouBD, etc., and clipping
file at the NYPL Music Division, Lincoln Center, New York City)

Scott, Hazel Dorothy

b. 11 June 1920 in Port of Spain, Trinidad; d. 2 October 1981 in New
York, New York. Classical and jazz pianist, arranger and composer.
Hazel Scott moved with her family to Harlem when she was four
years old. Her father was an English professor and her mother a
talented musician who played saxophone in Lil Hardin
Armstrong's All-Girl Orchestra. Hazel was a child prodigy and at
eight was accepted as a student by Paul Wagner of the Juilliard
School. When her mother organized her own Alma Long Scott's
All-Girl Band in 1933, Hazel played piano and trumpet, and she
made her first appearance on Broadway in "Sing Out the News" in
1938. She made her Carnegie Hall debut in December, 1940,
playing both straight classics and her own jazz spin-offs on them,
for which she became well-known. She married Harlem politician
and U.S. Representative Adam Clayton Powell, Jr. in 1945 and
during the 1960s she lived in Paris, France. She made many
recordings and numerous appearances on Broadway, films, radio
and television, continuing to play in night clubs until her death in
1981. Her compositions include original boogie woogie pieces, spin-
offs on the classics, and more serious works in a hybrid style. Most
have not been located in her own manuscript, but appear on concert
programs and published transcriptions made from her recordings.

Solo:
Caribbean Fete, ca. 1940; no ms.; performed on concerts by Hazel
    Scott; program located at the New York Public Library
    Lincoln Center Music Research Center; four movements com-
    posed "against the colorful background of the Carnival in
    Trinidad marking the last three days preceding Ash
    Wednesday and ushering in Lent."
    1. "Dame Lorraine," using a traditional melody from the
        Sunday night parade of the Mummers' opening

Carnival.

2. "Castellan," based on the Spanish Waltz, heard at Monday night Carnival parties.

3. "Paseo-Careso," better known as the *Calypso in D Minor*, bringing the Carnival to a close and leading without a break to:

4. "Ash Wednesday," entering the cathedral to celebrate mass.

Five Piano Solos from Boogie Woogie to the Classics, c. 1943; transcribed and edited by Morris Feldman and published by Leeds Music Corporation. (Copy located at New York Public Library, among others.)

1.*Hazel's Boogie Woogie*; 6 pp.; C Major, 2/2 "Fast Boogie Woogie Tempo"; continuous L.H. eighth note boogie pattern with ornamented R.H. melody. Moderately difficult.

2. *Two Part Invention in a Minor, by J.S. Bach;*4 pp; C Major, 2/2 "Fast"; after an eighteen measure introduction, Bach's invention is played straight about half-way through; then it evolves into a jazz version of itself. Moderately difficult.

3. *Prelude in C-sharp Minor by S. Rachmaninoff*; 5 pp.; C-sharp Major, 4/4; slow six-measure introduction from the opening of Rachmaninoff's *Prelude;* tempo switches to fast, and various motives from the *Prelude* are developed in jazz idiom. Difficult.

4. *Hungarian Rhapsody no. 2 in C-sharp Minor by Franz Liszt;* 6 pp.; C-sharp Minor(and D-flat and A-flat majors), 4/4; fifteen-measure slow introduction from Liszt's Rhapsody before taking off in fast jazz development of other sections. Difficult.

5. *Dark Eyes;* 3 pp.; D Minor, 4/4 "Slowly (with feeling)" two pages of classical rhapsodic style, followed by a page in "Medium Boogie Woogie Tempo." Moderately difficult.

Selected Bibliography:

Ledbetter, Les. "Hazel Scott, 61, Jazz Pianist, Acted in Films, on Broadway." *New York Times* (3 October 1981).

"Hep Hazel." *Newsweek* (29 November 1843).

(ASCAP, Handy, SouBD, and the NYPL Lincoln Center Music Division clipping files)

Simmons, Margo Nelleen

b. 26 June 1952 in Nashville, Tennessee. Flutist, professor, and composer. She attended the Putney School in Vermont on a four-year scholarship, studying flute and dance. At Antioch College in Ohio, she participated in the Education Abroad Program, traveling and performing in Holland, Spain, Morocco, Senegal, Ghana, Uganda, and Ethiopia during 1972–73. She completed her B.A. degree in music at Antioch in 1977, having been a member (flutist, dancer, composer) of the performing ensemble, The Pyramids, from 1971-1978. Her M.A. and Ph.D. in composition were completed at the University of California at San Diego in 1982 and 1987, respectively. She has taught at University of California at San Diego, the University of Ottowa in Ontario, Canada, and since 1987, at Hampshire College in Amherst, Massachusetts. Her honors include graduate fellowships and a Martin Luther King Award from UC San Diego, a Hewlett-Mellon Summer Research Grant for composition in 1989, and a commission to write a work for the Hampshire College Chorus in 1991. Her works have been selected for inclusion at UC San Diego's "Soundshapes" Contemporary Music Festival in 1983 (*Obeisance* for soprano and chamber ensemble) and the Conference on Women in Music at San Francisco State University in 1981 (*Trichotomy* for flute, clarinet and contrabass). Her works also include *Three Dream Songs* (1981–82) for soprano, flute, and contrabass, *Remembrance* (1984) for brass septet, *Dreaming Pair* (1984) for guitar solo, *Still Light* (1986) for chorus and percussion on texts by T. S. Eliot, "*Is This Real*" (1986) for contralto and chamber ensemble, *Three Pieces for Solo Flute* (1989) and her Ph.D. dissertation, *Distant Images of Time and Voice* (1987) for orchestra, chorus, soprano, contralto, and baritone soloists on texts by Jorge Luis Borges. Inquiries may be directed to the composer at Hampshire College, School of Humanities and Arts, Amherst, Massachusetts, 01002.

Solo:

> *For Jock*, 1985, solo piano transcription of a quintet for alto flute, alto clarinet, viola, cello, and contrabass, composed in 1983; transcribed and performed by pianist John MacKay at a Five College Composers Concert, Amherst, Massachusetts, in November 1987; 10 min.; atonal, changing meters, "Graceful" (quarter = 60-70); composer's note: "the juxtaposition of dynamic and static temporal conditions is basic to the conception of this composition"; intensely expressive and lyric; sustained notes, held and/or trilled, surrounded by swirls of faster groups, repeated notes accelerating and

slowing, tremolos on intervals of third, tritone, seventh, etc.; layers of activity involving polyrhythms; in two sections without a break, the first building in movement, dynamics and agitation; the second, (quarter = 36-40) very sustained, and static, gradually returning to the graceful motion of the opening; each section contains a duet passage between two lyrical lines; a quiet ending; no inside-piano techniques. Complex and difficult.

(Composer)

Smith, Irene Britton

b. n.d. in Chicago, Illinois. Pianist, educator, and composer. Smith pursued her avocation as a composer alongside a successful career as an elementary school teacher specializing in the Phonovisual approach to teaching reading. She graduated from Wendell Phillips High School and the Chicago Normal School, and holds the B.Mus. degree in theory and composition from the American Conservatory (1943) where she studied with Stella Roberts and Leo Sowerby. She did graduate work in composition at the Juilliard School with Vittorio Giannini for a year before completing her M.Mus. at De Paul University (1956) under Leon Stein. She also studied with Nadia Boulanger at the American Conservatory at Fontainebleau, France, as well as with Irving Fine at Tanglewood Music School in Massachusetts. Her works are lyrical and tonal, written in a conservative, neo-classical style. They include a *Sinfonietta* in three movements for full orchestra (1956), several choral works, chamber and solo works, and spiritual arrangements. In *Dream Cycle* (1947), she set poems of Paul Laurence Dunbar in a cycle of four art songs. Some of her works may be requested from her through the Center for Black Music Research at Columbia College, Chicago, 600 S. Michigan Ave., Chicago, IL 60605 (312) 663-9462.

Solo:
Invention in Two Voices, 1940.
Passacaglia and Fugue in C sharp Minor, 1940.
Two Short Preludes for Piano, 1953:
1. "Prelude no. 1," in process of revision; 4 pp. 3 min.; E-flat Major, 4/4; smoothly flowing counterpoint; begins with fifteen-measure melody imitated exactly at the octave below in canon; the two voices are expanded, one by one, to five; the melody is then varied and developed in several ways: in five-part harmony, inverted in the

bass, in octaves, in D Major, etc.

2. "Prelude no. 2"; 2 pp., 2 min.; C Major, mixed meters, "Moderato"; angular and dissonant; a study in fifths and triads juxtaposed a minor second apart, gradually stretching to major second, minor third, and finally to octaves on C at the extremes of the keyboard; through-composed. Moderate.

Variations on a Theme from MacDowell, 1947; eight variations with transitional development.

Ensemble:

Reminiscence for Violin and Piano, 1941.

Sonata for Violin and Piano, 1947; 26 pp., 15 min; first performed by Gregory Walker and Helen Walker-Hill in February 1990 at the Denver Public Library; three movements. Moderately difficult (see individual movements, below).

I. "Allegro cantabile - Allegro di molto": B-flat Minor, 4/4; form A B C A B Coda; contrasts broadly flowing contrapuntal cantabile section with mischievously playful sections in A Major (on return, in B flat Major); a middle section in E Minor is also flowing and expressive. Moderately difficult.

II. "Andante (con sentimento)": D flat Major, 3/4; serenely lyrical and expressive, with a livelier middle section in G Major. Moderate.

III. "Vivace": B-flat Major, 2/4; playful and leggiero, with a slower, tranquil middle section. Moderately difficult.

(Composer)

Solomon, Joyce Elaine

b. 11 May 1946 in Tuskegee, Alabama. Pianist, teacher and composer. Joyce Solomon grew up in Columbia, South Carolina, attended public schools there and began to study piano privately at age seven. She also played clarinet in the high school band and distinguished herself in science, winning a prize at a National Science Fair. She received a scholarship to study chemistry at Vassar College, Poughkeepsie, New York, minoring in piano with Gwendolyn Stevens and Ruslana Antonowicz. She completed her B.A. degree in 1968. She received a Master of Arts in Teaching degree in 1971 from Rutgers University, New Jersey, where she studied piano with Samuel Dilsworth-Leslie and composition with

Robert Moews. She then taught for two years at Booker T. Washington High School in Columbia, South Carolina, and Knoxville College in Tennessee, before completing a second Master of Fine Arts degree in composition at Sarah Lawrence College in 1975. There she studied composition and electronic music under Meyer Kupferman and Joel Spiegelman. She continued graduate studies at Teachers College- Columbia University, studying at the Columbia-Princeton Electronic Music Center with Vladimir Ussachevsky and Mario Davidovsky and receiving her Ed.D. from Columbia University in 1982. She has taught at the Brooklyn Music School and St. Joseph's College in Brooklyn, New York, St. Johns University in Jamaica, New.York, and in New York City at the Borough of Manhattan Community College, Henry Street Music School, Queens College, and the Harlem School of the Arts. Her husband is percussionist Wilson Moorman. She is a member of the American Society of Composers, Authors and Publishers, College Music Society, American Society of Composers, and Kappa Delta Pi. In 1989, she received a grant from Vassar College for a year's time-out to compose. The same year, she was one of five winners in the Detroit Symphony Afro-American Composers' Competition for her orchestral work, *The Soul of Nature*. (1975). Her solo, chamber, and vocal compositions have been performed by numerous groups including the Brooklyn Philharmonic Chamber Ensemble, LonGar Ebony Ensemble, Woodhill Players, and Triad Chorale of New York City. In 1990, she was commissioned by the Plymouth Chorus and Symphony Orchestra of Minneapolis, Minnesota, to write a piece for chorus and orchestra, *In Time of Silver Rain*, which was performed in February 1991. Solomon's compositional approach emphasizes both sound and organization, and is frequently twelve-tone. Her works are cerebral and very tightly constructed, at times minimalistic, pointillistic, or jazzy. The piano works explore the possibilities of the instrument, using inside-piano techniques. Her works can be obtained through the composer at 789 Coney Island Ave., Brooklyn, N.Y. 11218.

Solo:

> *Piano Suite,* 1974, premiered at Sarah Lawrence College Music Workshop, Bronxville, N.Y., 1974; 12 pp., 8 min.; nine miniatures composed in twelve-tone technique while studying with Meyer Kupferman; succinct and economical. Moderately difficult (see cross rhythms in V).
>
> > I. "Prelude"; 4/4, "Allegretto"; tiny (seven measures) three part form in two voices; off-beat three-note phrases in sixteenths.

II. "Grief"; 4/4, "Lento"; expressive, symmetrical three part form, three-note rhythmic motive recurs.

III. "3/8 Meets 2/8"; alternating 3/8 and 2/8 meters, "Allegro."

IV. "Introspection"; unmeasured "Adagio"; starts with expressive R.H. melodic line against chordal L.H., changing to both melodic lines.

V. "Cross Rhythms"; 3/4, "Moderato"; two melodic parts in constantly changing cross rhythms of all kinds.

VI. "Verticals"; 2/2, "Allegro"; chords, as name implies, made up of elements of the row; simple rhythmic patterns changing every two measures

VII. "Fugue"; 4/4, "Moderato"; 2 and 1/2 pp. (first of set longer than 1 p.); three voices; subject features three-note groups of sixteenths, like the "Prelude."

VIII. "Afterthought"; 4/4, "Allegro vivace"; hurried little (six measures) appendage to the "Fugue."

IX. "Toccata"; 1 and 1/2 pp.; 3/4, "Allegro"; rapid sixteenths scurry, hands together, to the conclusion of the set.

A Summer Afternoon in South Carolina, 1983, premiered at the Harlem School of the Arts Music Series, New York City, 1984, and also performed by Dennis Moorman at the Henry Street Music School, New York City, in 1985, and Lilan Parrot at the Brooklyn Music School in 1989; 15 pp, 15 min.; a programmatic sonata in three movements; compositional technique is a variant of twelve-tone; pedal precisely marked by composer. Difficult.

I. "Adagio"; 3/4, quarter = 40; a three part theme features languid R.H. melody against L.H. tone clusters; middle part inverts intervals of melody; variants on this thematic material, first ornamented, then in two-part invention style, then in solid, vertical groups accelerating to a cluster played with both arms and held; return to Tempo I and opening theme briefly, before accelerating again to concluding five-note clusters; no break, "attaca":

II. "Moderato"; 5/4, (quarter = 66); melodic material from first movement; sounds like a continuation of it; note values decrease, accelerating to a motoric repetition in high register, leading to an "Adagio" played entirely with arm clusters and inside-piano strumming; returns to motoric repetitions in high register before petering out; closes with recall of melodic motives in original note values; progressive dissolving (breaking of solid units) or congealing (solid vertical clusters) of sound is typical of Solomon's style.

III. "Allegro moderato"; 11/8, etc., (quarter = 152); playful, skipping effect of this movement created by two-note slurred motives passed back and forth between the hands, repetitions of patterns, and odd lengths of measures; initial passage returns periodically, like a rondo refrain; episodes feature first movement's intervallic motives in repeated patterns using imitation, inversion, diminution, augmentation, solid clusters, etc.; movement ends with motive in its original form, quoted exactly from the beginning of the first movement. (This movement is published in *Black Women Composers: A Century of Piano Music*, see Appendix 1.)

Variations on a Theme, 1971, premiered at Rutgers University Composers' Forum, 1971; 9 pp., 8 min.; most serial in sound of all her works, similar to Webern in his exploration of the expressive possibilities of serial techniques; applies set theory to intervallic cells; extremely cohesive and symmetrical (the last movement is, in fact, an inversion of the first); variation through transposition, rhythm, tempo, articulation, and expressive changes; pedal precisely marked. Difficult.

Theme. "Larghetto"; two phrases, six and seven measures long, respectively; motives include five-note clusters, three-note triplet groups, closing with two long-held five-note clusters, repeated in a mournful swaying refrain.

Variation I. "Moderato"; theme transposed up a third; some motives doubled in speed.

Variation II. "Andante"; transposed down a tritone; rolled clusters lend accelerating effect from preceding variations.

Variation III. "Spritely"; transposed down a minor third; R.H. clusters broken upward and slurred in two-note groups.

Variation IV. "Andante"; 6/8; in original key, completing a subset of first four variations; clusters broken downward and held, giving drooping, sad effect.

Variation V. "Moderato"; 6/8; more breaking up of cluster motives but theme's structure still clear; playful.

Variation VI. "Largo"; 3/4; motive now in single-note

triplets.

Variation VII. "Presto"; 4/4; clusters in single-note sixteenths, fast and mischievous; this variation marks the
maximum in break-up and distortion of motives.

Variation VIII. "Largo"; similar to VI, starts gradual return to original form of theme; uses different combina-
tions of notes from original clusters.

Variation IX. "Andante"; 6/4; continuation of exploration
of subsets of five-note clusters, this time tied and held
together.

Variation X. "Spritely"; groups and intervals re-forming
into recognizable clusters.

Variation XI. "Andantino (swinging)"; transposed a minor
third down; now back to five-note clusters, the concluding swaying held notes have regained their original
mournful character.

Variation XII. "Larghetto"; retrograde of Theme.

A Young Black Woman's Impressions of New York City, 1976,
premiered at the International Student House, New York
City, 1977; 11 pp., 8 min.; a suite of pieces with descriptive
titles - Solomon's most obviously programmatic set; colorful
effects; use of jazz. Moderately difficult.

1. "The Streets of New York"; unmeasured, "Allegro con
moto"; L.H. repeats same motoric staccato sixteenth-
note pattern throughout; R.H. imitates street noises
with scurrying sixteenths, honking groups of seconds,
and arm clusters.

2. "My Complaining Neighbors"; 4/4, "Adagio"; suggestions
of a blues bass, accented grace groups, inside-piano
strumming and arm clusters.

3. "After Dusk in the Upper West 90s"; unmeasured,
"Andante"; L.H. a lazy, walking blues bass line, shifting back and forth from major five-note scale pattern to
minor "blue" pattern; R.H. comes in with a few jazz
chords; suddenly, mood shifts to fast, loud and brassy,
before settling back down to the lazy bass line at end.

4. "Lincoln Center at Performance Time"; unmeasured; ran-
dom tuning-up orchestra sounds; juxtaposed fragments
from different tunes in different keys.

5. "The African Diplomatic Parties"; imitations of buzzing
of conversations and background "vamping" on the keyboard.

6. "A Serial Disco"; steady beat and repetitive riffs of disco
dance music.

      7. "A Cacophony of Sounds . . . New York City"; 4/4; a quodlibet of juxtaposed familiar tunes: "There's No Business Like Show Business," "La Cucaracha," etc.

Ensemble:

Among the Snow-capped Peaks, string quartet, piano, percussion, 1976, premiered at the International Student House, New York City, 1977.

Fantasy for Violin and Piano, 1978, premiered at the Museum of the City of New York, 1982; 16 pp., 8 min.; in one unbroken movement with several sections: "Andante," "Adagio," "Allegro vivace," and "Moderato" (return of material similar to beginning section); the instruments share and exchange motivic material; each has a solo cadenza. Difficult.

Oceana, piano, bass, flute, bass clarinet, percussion, 1978.

One Day In . . . , piano and percussion, 1985, written for husband, percussionist Wilson Moorman and premiered at the Third Street Music School, New York City, 1985; 41 pp., 22 min.; four movements; layers of sound; spare and minimalistic. Difficult.

      1. "Fall"; for piano and timpani; piano flurries of sixteenths in low register imitates timpani glissandi; long timpani solo; also uses drum sticks hitting on bowl.

      2. "Winter"; for piano, vibraphone, and glockenspiel; opens with twelve-tone row stated solo by vibraphone, then glockenspiel, then piano; movement built on motives from this row; inside-piano techniques, crystalline sounds.

      3. "Spring"; for piano, claves, wood block, maracas, vibraslap, ratchet, and cuica; weird, insect-like sounds; piano eventually enters with bird call-like patterns.

      4. "Summer"; for piano, high cymbal, low cymbal, snare drum, high tom-tom, low tom-tom, and bass drum; 12/8, "Allegro", (quarter = 112); piano begins with high steady eighths alternating an octave apart, with isolated percussion notes which become a steady syncopated dance rhythm; percussion and piano then exchange roles, and the piano plays quartal triads in low register creating an unusual sonority, in syncopated rhythm, against steady percussion eighths, gathering in intensity to final arm clusters and glissandi; a solo drum set improvisation brings the work to a close.

Sonatina, piano, flute, cello, 1971, premiered at the

International Student House, 1977; 21 pp., 15 min.; serial
techniques applied to groups and motives. Difficult.
I. "Allegro"; 4/4; distinctive, two-measure theme features
sequencing of motives a half-step lower; theme appears
first in cello, then piano, like a fugue subject; at flute
entrance, however, it returns to cello, inverted; similar
imitation and exchange characterizes the other
movements.
II. "Andante con moto"; 4/4.
III. "Allegro"; 4/4; cello opens with a four-note motive
(resembling B A C H) in slow, expressive arco bowing
changing to sul ponticello on each note; after a pause,
the other instruments join in rapid sixteenth counterpoint including the four-note motive in diminution;
rhythmically and intervallically reminiscent of the
theme of the first movement.
Trio, oboe, tuba, piano, 1978.
Trio, electronic tape, piano and percussion, 1980.

(Composer, Cohen, *International Who's Who in Music* 11th Edition,
1988, *Who's Who in American Music Classical*, 1983.)

Taylor, Jeanetta

b. late-nineteenth century. Composer. She is listed with two piano
compositions in the Walter Whittlesey File of Black Musicians at
the Library of Congress Music Division. Only one of them is in the
LC holdings.

Solo:
Our Soldier Boys, March and Two Step, c. 1898 , dedicated to
the Teachers Beneficial Association of Washington, D.C.,
published by Henry White of 929 F Street N.W.,
Washington, D.C.; 3 pp.; C Major, 4/4, "Allegro con brio";
four-measure introduction to "March," consisting of two
repeated sixteen-measure sections, the second section's
melody marked by dotted rhythm; L.H. accompaniment in
marching oom-pah pattern; "Trio" has its own four-measure
introduction and two sections, the first quiet, sixteen
measures and the second doubled in octaves, thirty
measures; a "D.C. al Fine" rounds off the piece with the
"March." Moderate. (Copies available through Library of
Congress, call number M28.T.)

Onward March, no further information.

(LCWh)

Thomas, Blanche Katurah

b. 1885 in New York City; d. 23 August 1977 in New York City. Choral conductor, teacher, and composer. A graduate of the Juilliard School of Music, Thomas also studied at Westminster Choir College and Union Theological Seminary. She taught church school music at the Harlem Religious Training School and also at Hampton Institute, in Virginia. She won a prize in the 1928 Rodney Wanamaker Music Composition Contest for her song, "I Think of Thee," and Honorable Mention in 1931 for "I Am Troubled in Mind." In 1932 she founded the Thomas Negro Composers Study Group so that Harlem youth could hear the works of Negro composers. Its members gave yearly recitals, including works by Robert Nathaniel Dett, Noah Ryder, Harry Burleigh, Ethel Ramos-Harris, Lillian Evanti, Carlotta Thomas, Florence Price, and others. She composed a great deal of choral music. Her choral music and memorabilia are housed at the Schomburg Center for Research in Black Culture, 515 Malcolm X Blvd., New York, N.Y. 10037-1801.

Solo:

Plantation Songs in Easy Arrangements for the Piano, c. 1937 by G. Schirmer, publisher; teaching arrangements of twelve spirituals with brief comments on the background of each spiritual, rhythmic exercises, scales, and list of musical terms. Very easy. (Copies located at Library of Congress, call number M1378.T39P4, and the Schomburg Center for Research in Black Culture, see above.)
1. "Go down, Moses"
2. "Steal Away to Jesus!"
3. "Swing Low, sweet Chariot"
4. "Lord, I Want to be a Christian in my heart"
5. "We are climbing Jacob's ladder"
6. "I ain't goin' to study war no more"
7. "I'm a-rollin' thro' an unfriendly world"
8. "I'm troubled in mind" (Variations)
9. "Were you there when they crucified my Lord?"
10. "I've got a robe"
11. "Tryin' to make heaven my home"
12. "Go tell it on the mountain"

(Carter, Schomburg Center for Research in Black Culture, LCC)

Tilghman, Amelia

b. ca. 1850 in Washington, D.C.; d. n.d., n.p. Singer, teacher, journalist, poet, and composer. Tilghman graduated from the Normal Department of Howard University in 1871, and taught for fourteen years in that city. For several years she concertized as a singer, appearing with Madam Selika, Nellie Brown and other prominent singers in Washington, New York, and at the Sangerfest in Louisville, Kentucky. She produced the cantata, *Queen Esther*, (presumably Handel's?) in Washington's Lincoln Hall in 1882, complete with orchestra and costumes, training the chorus of one hundred voices herself and taking the lead. She suffered a serious accident in 1882 while in Saratoga Springs, New York, on a singing engagement, when a brick fell from a scaffolding while she was passing underneath and fractured her skull. She attended the Boston Conservatory of Music to study methods of teaching piano, and later taught in Montgomery, Alabama, and at the Howe Institute in Louisiana. In 1886, while teaching music in Montgomery, she began the publication of the *Musical Messenger*, the first musical magazine published by a Negro. After her return to Washington by 1891, she continued publishing the magazine with the help of Lucinda Bragg Adams. In addition to the piano piece described below, a sacred song with piano and violin accompaniment, "Come See the Place Where the Lord Hath Lain," published in Washington in 1903, is located at the Moorland-Spingarn Research Center, Howard University, Washington, D.C. 20059 (202) 806-7480 (call number JEM 30.475).

Solo:

> *Hiawatha March*, c. 1903, dedicated to the Coleridge-Taylor Choral Society, published for the author by Sanders & Stayman Company, Washington, D.C.; 4 pp.; D Major, 4/4; eight-measure introductory "Allegro" and four sections: "Wedding March," "Death of Minnehaha," "Burial of Minnehaha," and "Hiawatha's Farewell"; each section contains two or three sixteen-measure subsections with new or related melodic material; "Hiawatha's Farewell" recalls thematic material from "Death of Minnehaha"; features big chords, octaves, dotted and triplet rhythms and melody transposed to bass. Moderate. (Copy available from Moorland-Spingarn Research Center, see above.)

(Majors, Mossell, Scruggs, SouBD)

Tucker, Rosina Harvey Corrothers, see Corrothers-Tucker, Rosina Harvey

Williams, Mary Lou

b. Mary Elfrida Scruggs 8 May 1910 in Atlanta, Georgia; d. 28 May 1981. Jazz pianist, arranger and composer. When she was around five years old, her family moved to Pittsburgh. Her mother played spirituals and ragtime, and Mary started to play piano at age two and one-half. While still in grade school, she began earning money by performing at parties, and in her teens, was touring with bands. She learned her craft by watching musicians like Jack Howard, Art Tatum, Don Redman, Buck Washington, Lovie Austin and Andy Kirk. She married John Williams, alto and baritone saxophone player with Kirk's band and was a member herself from the 1920s to 1941. She then began her own highly successful band, and was an arranger for many of the other great band leaders: Benny Goodman, Louis Armstrong, Duke Ellington, Cab Calloway, and others. Her *Zodiac Suite* was performed by the New York Philharmonic in 1946. She received two Guggenheim grants for her jazz compositions, and honorary degrees from Fordham, Boston and Loyola Universities, and Manhattan, Bates, and Rockhurst Colleges. She converted to Catholicism in 1956, and temporarily ceased performing. In 1964 she founded the Pittsburgh Jazz Festival, teaching in Pittsburgh's Catholic High School for a brief period. She also served on the faculty of Duke University from 1976 until her death. Her compositions include sacred choral music, orchestra and chamber music and many piano pieces. Her three masses were composed in 1966, 1968 and 1970. The last, *Mary Lou's Mass*, was performed on numerous occasions. Copies of the two collections listed below are located at the Library of Congress, the New York Public Library, and may also be in other libraries accessible to interlibrary loan.

Solo:

    Five Piano Solos, c. 1941 by publisher, Leeds Music Corporation. Moderately difficult. (Library of Congress, call number M22.W644P4; NYPL, call number 786-W.)

        1. *A Mellow Bit of Rhythm* (with Herman Walder); 4 pp.; C Major, 2/2, "Medium Swing tempo"; steady L.H. stride bass in quarter notes, with syncopated R.H. melody and jazz seventh chords.

        2. *Toadie Toddle* (with Sharon Pease); 4 pp.; C Major, 2/2, "Moderato"; nine measure introduction; accompaniment

alternates stride bass in tenths, dotted eighth rhythms; R.H. melody in thirds.

3. *Scratchin' in the Gravel;* 4 pp.; G Major, 2/2, "Medium Swing Tempo"; L.H. stride accompaniment with bass in open tenth chords; elaborate figuration in the R.H. melody; key change to D-flat Major.

4. *Mary Lou Williams Blues;* 4 pp.; E-flat Major, 2/2, "Medium Blues tempo; L.H. accompaniment in walking tenths; R.H. melody with chords, octaves.

5. *Walkin' and Swingin';* 4 pp.; F Major, 2/2, "Bright"; L.H. stride accompaniment with bass in tenths, some walking tenths; rambling R.H. melody; many key changes .

Six Original Boogie Woogie Piano Solos, c. 1944 by publisher, Robbins Music Corporation. Moderately difficult. (Library of Congress, call number M25.W; NYPL call number Mu 786.4-W.)

1. *Special Freight;* 3 pp.; C Major, 2/2, "Medium Slow"; L.H. boogie accompaniment in solid fifths and sixths in quarter and eighth notes, also broken-octave running boogie bass, punctuated by terse, fragmented R.H. melody in thirds and single notes; "train" type toots and blue notes.

2. *Deuces Wild;;* 5 pp.; C major, 2/2, "Slow"; L.H. open tenth chords; rambling, elaborate R.H. melody.

3. *Twinklin';* 5 pp.; C major, 2/2, "Medium Tempo"; L.H. stride accompaniment in open tenth chords; R.H. similar to *Deuces Wild,* in up tempo.

4. *Bobo and Doodles ;* 6 pp.; F Major, 2/2, "Medium Tempo"; rambling walking boogie bass; R.H. variety of melody and chords, humorous grace note-ornamented repeated notes; shifts to D-flat major.

5. *The Duke and the Count ;*3 pp; F major, 2/2, "Medium Tempo"; L.H. broken-octave boogie bass ostinato; R.H. terse, repeated motive melody.

6. *Chili Sauce;* 4 pp.; F Major, 2/2, no indication; L.H. stride accompaniment with open tenth chords changes to broken-octave boogie bass; melody features chains of repeated motives with shifting strong beats.

Numerous other pieces are recorded, but written transcriptions have not been located. These are listed in Cohen:

Camel Hop
Cloudy
The Devil
Dirge Blues

Easy Blues
Froggy Bottom
A Fungus Amungus
In the Land of Oo-bla-dee
The Jumper Tree
Little Joe from Chicago
Miss D.D.
Night Life
Pretty-eyed Baby (song by that title at the Library of Congress)
Roll Em

Ensemble:
Zoning Fungus II, two pianos, bass and drums (Cohen).

Selected Bibliography:
Handy, D. Antoinette. "Conversation with Mary Lou Williams: First Lady of the Jazz Keyboard." *The Black Perspective in Music* 8, no. 2 (Fall 1980):194–214.
(ASCAP, Cohen, Handy, SouBD, etc.)

Appendix 1

Available Published
Piano Music

Published songs and choral music are not included.

Black Women Composers: A Century of Piano Music (1893–1990).
Compiled and edited by Helen Walker-Hill.
  Amanda Aldridge. "Prayer Before Battle," from *Four Moorish Pictures*, 1927.
  Mable Bailey, *Prankster*, 1986.
  Regina Harris Baiocchi. "Etude II" from *Two Piano Etudes*, 1978.
  Margaret Bonds. *Troubled Water*, 1967.
  Valerie Capers. "Blues for the Duke," "A Taste of Bass," and "Billie's Song," from *Portraits in Jazz*, 1976.
  Anna Gardner Goodwin. *Cuba Libre March*, 1897.
  Betty Jackson King. "Spring Intermezzo," from *Four Seasonal Sketches*, 1955.
  Viola Kinney. *Mother's Sacrifice*, 1909.
  Tania León. *Preludes nos. 1 and 2*, 1966.
  Lena Johnson McLin. *A Summer Day*, 1970s.
  Dorothy Rudd Moore. *A Little Whimsy*, 1982.
  Undine Smith Moore. *Before I'd be a Slave*, 1953.
  Julia Perry. *Prelude for Piano*, 1946.
  Zenobia Powell Perry. *Homage*, 1990.
  Florence B. Price. *Fantasie Negre*, 1929.
  Philippa Duke Schuyler. Third movement of *White Nile Suite*, 1964.
  Joyce Solomon. Third movement of *A Summer Afternoon in South Carolina*, 1984.
  Mary Lou Williams. *Special Freight*, 1944.
Hildegard Publishing Company, Box 332, Bryn Mawr, Pennsylvania 19010. (215) 649-8649. Scheduled for publication in 1992.

Margaret Bonds.
    Solo:
        Troubled Water
Sam Fox Publishing Company, 170 N. E. 33rd Street, Ft. Lauderdale, Florida 33334. (305) 563-1844.

Avril Coleridge-Taylor.
    Solo:
        All Lovely Things
        Concert Etude
        Evening Song
        The Garden Pool
        In Memoriam
        Just as the Tide was Flowing, Berceuse and Nocturne
        Meditation 1
        Pastorale
        Rhapsody for Pianoforte, Op. 174
        Sussex landscape
        Two Short Pieces for Piano
    Piano and flute:
        Crepuscule d'une nuit d'été
        Fantaisie Pastorale
        Idylle
        Impromptu in A Minor, Op. 33
        A Lament
    Piano and violin:
        Fantasie
        Romance
    Piano and cello:
        Reverie
    Piano and Orchestra:
        Concerto in F Minor for Piano and Orchestra (for rent)
(Mostly manuscript facsimiles) Boosey & Hawkes Music Publishers Limited, 295 Regent Street,London, England W1R 8JH. (71) 580-2060. (Allow several months for delivery.)

Betty Jackson King.
    Solo:
        Aftermath
        Four Seasonal Sketches
        Mother Goose Parade
Jacksonian Press, Inc., P. O. Box 1556, Wildwood, N. J. 08260. (609)729-6677.

Tania León.
   Solo:
      Momentum
      Rituál
   Piano and percussion:
      A La Par
   Piano and flute:
      Pet's Suite
   Piano, flute, clarinet, cello, and violin:
      Parajota Delaté
   Piano and orchestra:
      Concerto Criollo
      Kabiosile
Peer-Southern Concert Music. Sole Distributor: Theodore Presser
Company, Presser Place, Bryn Mawr, Pennsylvania 19010. (215) 527-
4242.

Dorothy Rudd Moore:
   Solo:
      Dream and Variation
      A Little Whimsy
   Piano and violin:
      Three Pieces for Violin and Piano
   Piano and Cello:
      Dirge and Deliverance
   Piano and Clarinet:
      Night Fantasy
   Piano, violin, and cello:
      Trio no. 1
American Composers Alliance. Composers Facsimile Editions. 170 West
74th Street, New York, N.Y. 10023. (212) 362-8900.

Julia Perry
   Piano and orchestra:
      Concerto in Two Uninterrupted Speeds (manuscript facsimile)
      Concerto no. 2 (manuscript facsimile)
   Piano, percussion, and harp:
      Homunculus C.F.
Peer-Southern Concert Music. Sole Distributor: Theodore Presser
Company, Presser Place, Bryn Mawr, Pennsylvania 19010. (215) 527-
4242.

Appendix 2

Ensemble Instrumentation

The titles in boldface are known to be available.

Two Instruments

Two pianos:
    Jean Butler:
        Dance Suite
        Maria's Rags
        Mermaid's Aria
    Jacqueline Butler Hairston:
        Theme and Variations on "In That Great Getting-Up Morning"
    Helen Eugenia Hagan:
        Concerto in C Minor, arr. for two pianos
    Delores Martin:
        La Mer Turbulente
    Undine Smith Moore:
        Romance
    Florence Price:
        Annie Laurie
        Fantasie Negre
        Silent Night
        Concerto in One Movement, arr. for two pianos
        Three Little Negro Dances, arr. for two pianos:
        "Hoe Cake"
        "Rabbit Foot"
        "Ticklin' Toes"
    Gertrude Robinson:
        Seven Scenes with Balabil

Piano and Violin:
    Avril Coleridge-Taylor:
        Fantasie
        Romance
    Betty Jackson King:
        A Cycle of Life
    Dorothy Rudd Moore:
        Three Pieces for Violin and Piano
    Julia Perry:
        Violin (or viola?) Sonata
    Zenabia Powell Perry:
        Fantasy
    Florence Price:
        By Candlelight
        The Deserted Garden
        Elfentanz
        Mellow Twilight
        Playful Rondo
    Irene Britton Smith:
        Reminiscence for Violin and Piano
        Sonata for Violin and Piano
    Joyce Solomon:
        Fantasy for Violin and Piano

Piano and Cello:
    Margaret Bonds:
        I Want Jesus to Walk With Me
        Troubled Water
    Avril Coleridge-Taylor:
        Reverie
    Jeraldine Herbison:
        An Invention Upon an Airy Upland
        Fantasy in Three Moods, **for cello (or viola) and piano**
        Intermezzo, Op. 9
        Sonata no. 2, for Cello and Piano
    Dorothy Rudd Moore:
        Dirge and Deliverance
    Florence Price:
        Sonatine

Piano and flute:
    Mable Bailey:
        Kind-a Blue

Avril Coleridge-Taylor:
Crepuscule d'une nuit d'été
Fantaisie pastorale
Idylle
Impromptu in A Minor
A Lament
Tania León:
Pet's Suite
Undine Smith Moore:
Three Pieces for Flute (or Clarinet) *and piano*
Gertrude Robinson:
Moods I and II
Dedication to Ruth, Mary, and Martha
Dedication to Carson McCullers

Piano and Clarinet:
Regina Harris Baiocchi:
Chasé
Dorothy Rudd Moore:
Night Fantasy
Undine Smith Moore:
Three Pieces for Flute (or Clarinet) *and Piano*
Zenobia Powell Perry:
Sonatine

Piano and Saxophone:
Gertrude Rivers Robinson:
Moods

Piano and French Horn:
Zenobia Powell Perry:
Episodes I and II

Piano and percussion:
Tania León:
A la Par
Joyce Solomon:
One Day In . . .

Piano and marimba:
Lettie Beckon Alston:
Visions

Three Instruments

Piano, violin, and cello:
    Lettie Beckon Alston:
        Memories
    Jeraldine Herbison:
        Trio no. 3
    Dorothy Rudd Moore:
        Trio no. 1
    Undine Smith Moore:
        Soweto
    Ruth Norman:
        Capriccio
    Zenobia Powell Perry:
        Excursion

Piano, violin and oboe:
    Jeraldine Herbison:
        Nocturne
        Miniature Trio

Piano, violin and clarinet:
    Rachel Eubanks:
        Trio

Piano, cello and clarinet:
    Diana Greene:
        Trio
    Zenobia Powell Perry:
        Two Letters

Piano, cello and oboe:
    Diana Greene:
        Tragedies

Piano cello and flute:
    Undine Smith Moore:
        Afro-American Suite
    Joyce Solomon:
        Sonatina

Piano flute, and clarinet:
    Florence Price:
        Two Moods

Piano, flute, and oboe:
  Zenobia Powell Perry:
    Four Mynyms for Three Players

Piano, harp, and guitar:
  Alice McLeod Coltrane:
    Bliss: The Eternal Now

Piano, oboe, and tuba:
  Joyce Solomon:
    Trio

Piano, electronic tape, and percussion:
  Joyce Solomon:
    Trio

Four Instruments

Piano quartet:
  Jeraldine Herbison:
    Piano Quartet, Op. 18 no. 1

Piano, flute, violin, cello:
  Jeraldine Herbison:
    I Heard the Trailing Garments of the Night
    Introspection, Op. 8

Piano, clarinet, violin, cello:
  Diana Greene:
    Trilogy

Piano, flute, trumpet, bass:
  Diana Greene:
    Rigorisms II

Two pianos, bass, and drums:
  Mary Lou Williams:
    Zoning Fungus II

Five Instruments

Piano Quintet (strings):
> Margaret Bonds:
>> *Quintet in F Major*
> Florence Price:
>> *Quintet in E Minor*
> Gertrude Rivers Robinson:
>> *Quintet for Piano and Strings*

Piano, flute, bass clarinet, bass and percussion:
> Joyce Solomon:
>> *Oceana*

Piano, flute, clarinet, cello, violin:
> Tania León:
>> *Parajota Delaté*

Piano, 2 violins, cello, guitar:
> Jeraldine Herbison:
>> *Metamorphosis*

Six Instruments

Piano, string quartet, percussion:
> Joyce Solomon:
>> *Among the Snow-Capped Peaks*

Piano, flute, alto flute, oboe, B-flat clarinet, bassoon:
> Regina Harris Baiocchi:
>> *Chasé*

Indefinite number of players

Piano and brasses:
> Florence Price:
>> *Suite for Brasses and Piano*

Piano, woodwinds and percussion:
> Zenobia Powell Perry:
>> *Ships That Pass in the Night*

Piano, percussion and harp:
    Julia Perry:
        Homunculus C.F.

Piano and orchestra (see also two pianos):
    Lettie Beckon Alston:
        Fantasy for Piano and Orchestra
        The Integrated Concerto
    Avril Coleridge-Taylor:
        Concerto in F Minor for Piano and Orchestra
    Helen Eugenia Hagan:
        Concerto in C Minor **(see arr. for two pianos)**
    Margaret Harris:
        Concerto no. 1 for Piano and Orchestra ("North Sea Suite")
        Concerto no.2 for Piano and Orchestra
    Tania León:
        Concerto Criollo
        Kabiosile
        Tones
    Julia Perry:
        Concerto for Piano and Orchestra in Two Uninterrupted Speeds
        Concerto no. 2 for Piano and Orchestra
    Florence Price:
        Concerto for Piano and Orchestra in One Movement
        Rhapsody for Piano and Orchestra
    Philippa Duke Schuyler:
        Nile Fantasia

Appendix 3

Easy and Moderate Pieces for Teaching

Only those works which the author has located are listed. Availability is indicated in the composer entries in the catalog.

Very easy:

Margaret Bonds:
> *Lillian M. Bowles First Edition of 12 Easy Lessons and Exercises For The Piano*

Florence Price:
> (Numerous very easy beginning pieces at the U. of A. collection available in negative photocopy of mss.: "Autumn Echoes," "Brownies at the Seashore," "Brung, the Bear," "Climbing the Mountain," "The Froggie and the Rabbit," "Golden Corn Tassels," "Little pieces on black keys," "Little Pieces on white keys," "The "Nodding Poppies," "On higher ground," "On the Playground," "A Pleasant Thought," "Strong Men Forward," "Up and Down the Ladder .")
> Also:
> "Bright Eyes"
> "Cabin Song"
> *The Sea Swallow*

Blanche K. Thomas:
> *Plantation Songs in Easy Arrangements for the Piano*

Easy:
  Rosina Harvey Corrothers-Tucker:
    Untitled manuscript in "Tempo di Valse"
  Ruth Norman:
    The Tea Party"
  Zenobia Powell Perry:
    Piano Potpourri: "Vignette," "Orrin and Echoe," "Ties"
  Florence Price:
    The Gnat and the Bee
    The Old Boatman
    The Rose
    The Waltzing Fairy
  Philippa Duke Schuyler:
    Nine Little Pieces
    Three Little Pieces

Easy to Moderate:
  Valerie Capers:
    Portraits in Jazz: "Ella Scats the Little Lamb," "Billie's Song,"
      "Waltz for Miles," "Sweet Mr. Jelly Roll," "Blues for the
      Duke," "A Taste of Bass," "Satchmo"
  Augusta Geraldine McSwain:
    The Chase
  Ruth Norman:
    "Winter Days"
    "Tippy (my Teddy bear)"
    "The Swing"
  Zenobia Powell Perry:
    Piano Potpourri: "Teeta"
  Florence Price:
    The Butterfly
    The Goblin and the Mosquito
    A Sachem's Pipe
    Three Little Negro Dances:
    1 "Hoe Cake"
    2."Rabbit Foot"
    3. "Ticklin Toes"
    Were You There When They Crucified My Lord?

Moderate:
  Amanda Aldridge (Montague Ring):
    Bagdad Suite: "The Royal Guard," "The Garden Beautiful"
    Carnival Suite: "Harlequin," "Columbine"
    Mirette Serenade

Four Moorish Pictures: "Prayer Before Dawn," "Dance of the
   Slave Girls"
Three Pictures from Syria: "Beneath the Crescent Moon"
Mable Bailey:
   Dance
   Dialogue
   Prankster
Valerie Capers:
   Portraits in Jazz: "The Monk," "Cancion de Havana," "Bossa
      Brasilia"
Rachel Eubanks:
   Prelude for Piano
Rosina Harvey Corrothers-Tucker:
   Rio Grande Waltzes*
Betty Jackson King:
   Four Seasonal Sketches: "Spring Intermezzo"* "Autumn"*
   Mother Goose Parade*
Viola Kinney:
   Mother's Sacrifice*
Ida Larkins:
   Wild Flowers
Tania León:
   Ensayos sobre una Toccata*
   Homenaje a Prokofiev
   Preludes 1 ,"Sorpresa (Surprise)" and 2, "Pecera (Aquarium)"*
Augusta McSwain:
   Passacaglia in E Minor
   Rustic Dance
Dorothy Rudd Moore:
   A Little Whimsy
Undine Smith Moore:
   Scherzo
   Fugue in C Minor
   Romantic Young Clown
Ruth Norman
   Autumn
   "It's Raining"
Julia Perry:
   Prelude for Piano*
Zenobia Powell Perry:
   Blaize
   Homage*
   Piano Potpourri : "Jazz Notes," "Round and Round"
   Sonatina

Florence Price:
  *Arkansas Jitter**
  *At the Cotton Gin**
  *Bayou Dance**
  The Cotton Dance
  *Dance of the Cotton Blossoms**
  Dances in the Canebrakes:
  1. "Nimble Feet"*
  2. "Tropical Noon"
  3. "Silk Hat and Walking Cane"*
  Levee Dance
  Rocking Chair
Estelle Ricketts:
  Rippling Spring Waltz
Irene Britton Smith:
  "Prelude no. 2"
Jeanetta Taylor:
  *Talladega March**
Amelia Tilghman:
  *Hiawatha March**

* = Moderate to moderately difficult.

Chronology of Surviving Piano Works Before 1920

Pre-1900 information on music by black women:
- 16th century minstrel Theodora Gaines, composer of songs in Cuba.
- ca. 1870, singer Annie Pauline Pindell, 1834–1901, composed and published her song "Seek the Lodge Where the Red Men Dwell."
- 1885, publication of first surviving song which has been located: "Forgive," by Louise Smith, followed by "Old Blandford Church," 1886, by Lucinda Bragg, and "You Know," 1887, by Mrs. Sam Lucas.
- 1893, publication of Lawson Scruggs's *Women of Distinction* and Monroe Majors' *Noted Negro Women*, describing composers Mrs. J. E. Edwards, May Heyers, Mrs. N. A. R. Leslie, Mrs. Mary Sinclair, and Amelia Tilghman.
- 1894, publication of Mrs. N. F. Mossell's *The Work of the Afro-American Woman*, listing "Miss Estelle Rickets, Miss Bragg, Miss Tillman, Mrs. Yeocum and Mrs. Ella Mossell" as composers.

1893: Estelle D. Ricketts, *Rippling Spring Waltz*
1896: Frances Gotay (Sister Mary Seraphine), *La Puertorriqueña.*
1897: Anna Gardner Goodwin, *Cuba Libre March*
1898: Jeanetta Taylor, *Our Soldier Boys, March and Two Step*
1902: Rosina Harvey Corrothers-Tucker, *Rio Grande Waltzes*
——: Anna Gardner Goodwin, *Educational Congress March*
1903: Amelia L. Tilghman, *Hiawatha March*
1905: Ida Larkins, *Wild Flowers*
——: Josie Wilhelmina Roberts, *Talladega March*
1906: Mable E. Harding, *Farewell, Alma Mater*
1909: Viola Kinney, *Mother's Sacrifice*

1912: Helen Eugenia Hagan, *Concerto in C Minor*
1913: Amanda Aldridge (Montague Ring), *Three African Dances*
1919: ———, *Three Arabian Dances*

(Among the missing from this period: Florence Price's early works, Helen Eugenia Hagan's violin sonatas and piano pieces, and Nora Holt's compositions.)

Selected Bibliography

Ammer, Christine. *Unsung: A History of Women in American Music.* Westport, CT: Greenwood Press, 1980.

Baker, David N., Lida M. Belt, and Herman C. Hudson. "Undine Smith Moore." Chap. 7 in *The Black Composer Speaks*, 173–202. Metuchen, N. J.: Scarecrow Press, 1978.

Bonds, Margaret. "A Reminiscence." In *The Negro in Music and Art*, ed. by Lindsay Patterson, 190–193. New York: International Library of Negro Life and History, 1967.

Brown, Rae Linda. "The Orchestral Music of Florence B. Price (1888–1958): A Stylistic Analysis." Ph.D. diss., Yale University, 1987.

Cohen, Aaron. *International Encyclopedia of Women Composers*, 2d ed. 2 vols. New York: Books and Music, 1987.

Dannett, Sylvia. *Profiles in Negro Womanhood.* 2 vols. New York: Negro Heritage Library, 1966.

Green, Mildred Denby. *Black Women Composers: A Genesis.* Boston: Twayne Publishing Company, 1983.

Handy, D. Antoinette. *Black Women in American Bands and Orchestras.* Metuchen, N.J.: Scarecrow Press, 1981.

———."Conversations with Mary Lou Williams: First Lady of the Jazz Keyboard." *Black Perspective in Music* 8, no. 1 (Spring 1980):194–214.

Harris, Carl, Jr. "Conversations with Undine Smith Moore: Composer and Master Teacher." *Black Perspective in Music* 13, no. 1 (Spring 1985):79–85.

Jackson, Barbara Garvey. "Florence Price, Composer." *Black Perspective in Music* 5, no. 1 (Spring 1977):31–43.

MacAusian, Janna, and Kristan Aspen. "Price, Bonds, and Perry: Three Black Women Composers." *Hot Wire.* (September 1989):12–.

Majors, Monroe A. *Noted Negro Women, Their Triumphs and Activities.* Chicago: Donohue & Henneberry Printers, 1893.

McGinty, Doris E. "Conversations with Camille Nickerson: The Louisiana Lady." *Black Perspective in Music* 7, no. 1 (Spring 1979):81-90.

Patterson, Willis. *Anthology of Art Songs by Black American Composers.* Boston: E. B. Marks, 1977.

Roach, Hildred. *Black American Music: Past and Present,* 2 vols.. Malabar, Fl.: Crescendo, 1973, 1985.

Scruggs, Lawson A. *Women of Distinction.* Raleigh, N.C.: E. M. Uzzeli, 1893.

Southern, Eileen. *Biographical Dictionary of Afro-American and African Musicians.* 2d ed. Westport, CT: Greenwood Press, 1982.

———. *The Music of Black Americans: A History.* 2d ed. New York: W. W. Norton, 1983.

Talalay, Kathryn. "Philippa Duke Schuyler, Pianist/ Composer/ Writer." *Black Perspective in Music* 10, No. 1 (Spring 1982):43-68.

Tischler, Alice. "Margaret Bonds." "Dorothy Moore." In *Fifteen Black American Composers: A Bibliography of Their Works.* 37–58; 201–212. Detroit Studies in Music Bibliography, no. 45. Detroit: Information Coordinators, 1981.

Yuhasz, Sister Marie. "Black Composers and Their Piano Music." *American Music Teacher.* 19 (February/March 1970):24–25.

Williams, Ora. *American Black Women in the Arts and Social Sciences,* 2d. ed. Metuchen, N. J.: Scarecrow Press, 1978.

Selected Discography

The many jazz recordings by Valerie Capers, Alice McLeod Coltrane, Dorothy Donegan, Hazel Scott, and Mary Lou Williams are beyond the scope of this list and can be found listed elsewhere in jazz discographies. The recordings listed below are out of print in some cases, but may be possible to find in music libraries.

Amanda Aldridge (Montague Ring):
> *Three African Dances.* Orchestrated by Hale Smith from the piano
> score, and performed and recorded by the Black Music
> Repertory Ensemble in 1989 on *Black Music: The Written
> Tradition,* produced by the Center for Black Music Research,
> Columbia College, 600 S. Michigan Avenue, Chicago, IL 60605-
> 1996 (312) 663-1600 Ext. 559 or 560.

Margaret Bonds:
> *Troubled Water.* Recorded by Ruth Norman, pianist. Opus One, #39.
> Opus One Records, Box 604, Greenville, ME 04441.
> For spiritual arrangements for solo voice, see recordings by Leontyne
> Price, RCA-LSC2600 and RCA-LSC3183.
> For art songs, see *Art Songs by Black American Composers,* Willis
> Patterson, artistic director. Produced by the University of
> Michigan, School of Music, Ann Arbor, MI 48109. Stereo
> SM0015, 1981.

Jean Butler:
> *Maria's Rags, I, II.* Performed by Rees and Stoyanoff, duo-pianists,
> on *Music by American Women Composers.* Bravura Recordings
> BR1001 (Cassette)

Jacqueline Butler Hairston:
>   *A Change Has Got to Come.* London Philharmonic, William
>   Brown, tenor, and Barbara Jordan, narrator. Limited Edition
>   Recording by Columbia Records.
>   "Loving You." On *Andre Kostelanitz Plays Superman and Other
>   Hits..* Columbia Records.
>   *Satire.* Barbara Carroll, piano. United Artists Recording.

Tania León:
>   *Haiku.* Dance Theatre of Harlem Orchestra; with *Four Pieces for
>   Cello,* Michael Rudiakov, cellist; *I Got Ovah,* Johana, soprano,
>   Yolanda Liepa, piano, and Tom Goldstein, percussion; and
>   *Voices and Piccolo Flute,* Tania León, electronic tape. Opus
>   One,#101. (See Bonds, above, for address.)

Lena Johnson McLin:
>   *Glory, Glory, Allelulia.* Performed by Virginia Union Choir, Odell
>   Hobbs, conductor. Richmond Sound Stages, RSSWO 626.
>   *Sanctus.* Performed by Virginia Union Choir, Odell Hobbs, conduc-
>   tor. Gerald Lewis Records MC8806

Dorothy Rudd Moore:
>   *Dirge and Deliverance.* Kermit Moore, cello, Raymond Jackson,
>   piano. Performance Records, 1981. Available from Cespico
>   Records, Ltd., 1790 Broadway, New York, N.Y. 10019.
>   *From the Dark Tower.* Hilda Harris, mezzo-soprano, Wayne
>   Sanders, piano, and Kermit Moore, cello. Performance Records.
>   *Modes,* for string quartet. Opus One Records, forthcoming.
>   *Weary Blues,* see *Art Songs by Black American Composers,* under
>   Bonds

Undine Smith Moore:
>   *Afro-American Suite.* On *Contemporary Black Images in Music for
>   the Flute,* Trio Pro Viva: D. Antoinette Handy, flute, Ronald
>   Crutcher, cello, Gladys Perry Norris, piano. Eastern Recording
>   ERS 513, c. 1973.
>   *A Concert of Music by Undine Smith Moore.* Undine Smith Moore
>   Festival concert on 24 June 1990 at the Stevens Center for the
>   Performing Arts, Winston-Salem, North Carolina. Cassette
>   tape available from Simona Allen, c/o Delta Arts Center, 1151
>   E. 3rd st., Winston-Salem, N.C. 27101. Includes *Before I'd Be A
>   Slave* . Armenta Hummings, piano.*Soweto.* Elaine Campbell,
>   violin, Ronald Crutcher, cello, Joyce Johnson, piano; *Three
>   Pieces for Flute and Piano.* Janese Sampson, flute, and Monica

Otal, piano, plus art songs and choral works.

Lord, We Give Thanks to Thee. Choral works by Moore and Lena McLin, performed by the Virginia Union Choir, Odell Hobbs, conductor. Eastern Recording ERS-549, c.1976.

Undine Smith Moore Song Book. Virginia State College Concert Choir, Carl Harris, Jr., conductor. Richsound 4112 N10 c. 1975. Virginia State College, Box 352, Petersburg, VA 23803

Undine Smith Moore. An autobiographical lecture by the composer. Cambria Records C143. Available from Cambria Records and Publishing, Box 374, Lomita, CA 90717 (213) 831-1322.

Ruth Norman:

Molto Allegro, and *Prelude nos. 1 and 4 .* Performed by Ruth Norman, piano. Opus One # 35 and 39 (See Bonds, above).

Julia Perry:

Homunculus C.F. for percussion, harp and piano, performed by the Manhattan Percussion Ensemble, Paul Price, conductor. Composers Recordings, Inc. CRI-S252.

A Short Piece for Orchestra. Tokyo Imperial Philharmonic Orchestra, William Strickland, conductor. Composers Recordings, Inc. CRI-145.

Stabat Mater. Makiko Asakuro, mezzo-soprano, Japan Philharmonic Orchestra, William Strickland, conductor. Composers Recordings, Inc. CRI-133.

Florence Price:

Althea Waites Performs the Piano Music of Florence Price. Sonata in E Minor, The Old Boatman, Cotton Dance, Dances in the Canebrakes. Cambria Records C-1027 (Cassette Version CT-1027). Cambria Records and Publishing, Box 374, Lomita, CA 90717 (213) 831-1322.

For art songs, see *Art Songs by Black American Composers,* Willis Patterson, artistic director, University of Michigan, SM 0015 as well as *Lucille Fields Sings Songs by American Women Composers.* Cambria Records CD-1037 (Cassette Version CT-1037).

For spiritual arrangements, see Marian Anderson, Victor 1799; Isabella Davis, London LPS-182; Leontyne Price RCA-LSC-2600; and *Were You There When They Crucified My Lord,* Salli Terri with the Roger Wagner Chorale, Capitol Records, Inc., P8365)

Gertrude Rivers Robinson:
   Moods. Performed by Paul Stewart, saxophone, Deon Price, piano,
      on *Romantic Sax - Echosphere.* Cambria Records CT-1047
      (Cassette only). Cambria Records and Publishing, Box 374,
      Lomita, CA 90717 (213) 831-1322.

Index

About the Author

HELEN WALKER-HILL is also publishing an anthology of piano music, *Black Women Composers: A Century of Piano Music, 1893-1990*. Her articles have appeared in journals such as *American Music Teacher* and *Black Music Research Bulletin*. Her lecture/recital, "Rediscovered Heritage: The Music of Black Women Composers," has been featured on National Public Radio's "Morning Edition" and "Horizons" programs and was the subject of a United States Information Agency film for foreign distribution.